What Now?

"A well-written list of solid, common-sense advice. Convenient chapter organization allows readers to pick their problem and look it up! Easy to understand and down to earth."

Thomas W. Phelan, PhD
Author of the best-selling *1-2-3 Magic: The New 3-Step Discipline for Calm, Effective, and Happy Parenting*

"Rachel Biale offers wisdom, clarity and practical suggestions."

Jill Shugart, MFT
Former Director Nursery School

"... thoughtful solutions that can be reasonably implemented into practice."

Dr. Alan Shonkoff
Associate Clinical Professor of Clinical Neuropsychology

"... particularly helpful to new parents."

Dr. Bruce Linton
Psychologist, Founder of "Fathers' Forum," author of *Fatherhood: The Journey from Man to Dad*

"*What Now?* offers gently prescriptive advice for so many behavioral and emotional issues in childhood. . . . Parents will find them refreshing. Parenting is a journey, and this book provides a useful guide."

Robert A. Saul, MD
Professor of pediatrics, author of *Conscious Parenting: Using the Parental Awareness Threshold, Thinking Developmentally*, and other child-rearing titles

"Rachel Biale tackles parenting issues in a chronological and comprehensive way. The question-and-answer format is ideal. This is a must-have book for every parent and grandparent!"

Pam Siegel and Leslie Zinberg
Authors of *Grandparenting: Renew, Relive, Rejoice*

"*What Now?* is precisely what busy parents need in our fast-paced lifestyle of the new millennium! Parenting smoothly in the present will also result in later years becoming a bit more manageable. Rachel's steps provide a clear, compassionate path to everyone cohabitating peacefully!"

Gigi Gaggero
Author of *Food Fight for Parents of Picky Eaters*, a 2019 National Parenting Products Award Winner

"*What Now?* offers a fresh, balanced look at challenges faced by today's parents. The Q-&-A format is full of quick, easy-to-use parenting hacks, along with templates that help parents create books with children going through a difficult time."

Dr. Stefanie Naumann
Award-winning author of How Languages Saved Me: A Polish Story of Survival

What Now?

2-Minute Tips for Solving Common Parenting Challenges

by Rachel Biale

© Copyright 2020 Rachel Biale

ISBN 978-1-64663-059-2

Published by

◄ köehlerbooks™

3705 Shore Drive
Virginia Beach, VA 23455
800–435–4811
www.koehlerbooks.com

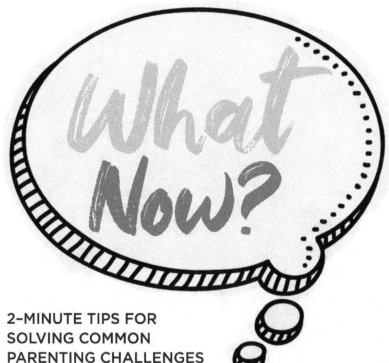

What Now?

**2-MINUTE TIPS FOR
SOLVING COMMON
PARENTING CHALLENGES**

Rachel Biale

VIRGINIA BEACH
CAPE CHARLES

For my kids, Noam and Tali: raising you has taught me everything in this book and so much more.
And in memory of our two Aninas, the grand one and the little one, both no longer in this world but always in my heart, guiding my life.

Table of Contents

I write this book as a mother, grandmother, and parenting counselor with over thirty-five years of experience. In more subtler ways, my parenting advice is also shaped by my own childhood, growing up in a kibbutz in Israel, where children were raised in collective Children's Houses. Communal responsibility, a level of independence unimaginable for contemporary American kids, and physical work were the hallmarks of my childhood. (If you are curious, I refer you to my book, *Growing Up Below Sea Level: A Kibbutz Childhood* published by Mandel Vilar Press.)

I am ever conscious of how challenging it is to be a parent. Nothing else in my life has been as rich, amazing, and, at the same time, humbling as raising our children. Parents today are bombarded with information: the confusion you often feel is not only justified but can also be paralyzing. I hope you will find the advice I offer useful, but do take it with a grain of salt: only some of it may be right for you.

Surely you will disagree with some of my views and recommendations. You may, on occasion, find them opinionated, too permissive, or too restrictive for your taste. That's good! These cases provide an opportunity for you to work through what aligns with your views and your family's situation, with thoughtful consideration and perhaps additional reading and consultation with friends or professionals. I also recognize that most of the advice in this book is based on an underlying assumption that your family is fortunate enough to have two parents, a safe home, stable employment and finances, and a network of family members and friends to support you. This is only for the sake of concision: I am *well aware* that this is not the case for many parents.

If you are a single parent, my hat's off to you. That in addition to parenting solo you are also able to read this book, let alone the preface, is amazing. If you are in a blended, multi-parent family or some other child-rearing configuration, you may have a bit more time that's free of caring for your child/ren. Still, the additional weight of piloting or co-piloting your kids' life emotionally, socially, financially, and logistically, is surely a big one. Whatever your specific circumstance, I am delighted you have found a few minutes to read this book and hope you'll adopt it as your parenting companion.

Finally, this book includes a lot of advice geared to parents in Jewish families. This is because a good part of it began as a parenting advice column in a Jewish community newspaper in the Bay Area. If you are not Jewish, you may skip certain chapters, but actually, I encourage you to read them. The underlying issues are likely to apply, with changes of terms and specifics, to your cultural tradition. Furthermore, if you are Christian, I think you'll find it illuminating to read a book where the majority Christian culture is *not* taken for granted. It will hopefully make you more attuned to and considerate of the experience of minorities in our country, be their status based on culture, religion, ethnic background, or gender identity.

PART I: Babies and Toddlers

I. Sleep, Soothing, Feeding, and Attachment

Getting Your Baby to Sleep Through the Night
(This is HARD, so this is a four-minute tip)

We are exhausted! Our seven-months-old baby is up four to six times a night, nursing up to half an hour each time. We need help getting the baby on a reasonable schedule before we lose our marbles.

Babies and sleep are almost always parents' top priority, and the advice you'll find (and get, even when you don't ask for it) is so varied and offered with such passion that it's practically impossible to figure out what to do. Let me begin with what often happens, willy-nilly or as a last resort: having your baby in your bed and nursing whenever she awakes, just to get her back to sleep and get a bit more rest yourself. As you may know, the American Academy of Pediatrics (AAP) recommends against bed-sharing, due to concerns about smothering infants and the possibly increased risk of SIDS (more research is needed). Furthermore, I know from the hundreds of parents I have counseled that often co-sleeping just doesn't work, especially if both parents go to work the next morning. You cannot get the quality of sleep needed to function in the adult world with its myriad duties and stresses.

I highly recommend you train your baby to sleep in their own crib (or co-sleeper bassinet). For the first three months, keep the crib adjacent to your bed (in your room, per the AAP recommendations). Thereafter, keep the crib in *the baby's* own room—if you have the space. Even a walk-in closet will work for a good while. This will improve and lengthen both your and the baby's sleep. A good time to start the sleep training is a week or two after you have moved the baby to their own room: it's easier to implement, especially in the middle of the night, once the baby is not in sight, sound, and smell range of you in your bed.

Sleep training works *best* when you structure it along these ABC building blocks:

A. Learning to fall asleep in the crib (not on the breast, in your arms, in a carrier, etc.)

B. Lengthening the sleep phases (and reducing nighttime nursing/feeding)

C. Learning to go back to sleep from light sleep/slight waking on their own.

When to start? Your baby is ready for gentle going-to-sleep training at around three months. Two fundamental steps taken now will become the building blocks of consistent bedtime routines and, later, sleeping through the night.

1. Help your baby attach to a "transitional object:" something strongly associated with the soothing of nursing, a bottle, and rocking. Get a small stuffed animal or buy a "lovie" (found in most baby stores). The AAP recommends having *nothing* in the crib, so after the baby is asleep, lean over (when the bassinet is by your bed) or tiptoe into their room and remove it. Have it handy so that you can put it back in your baby's hand when they awake in the middle of the night (more details below) and, again, once they've settled back to sleep, gently remove it. If your baby forms a strong attachment, then once they're out of the SIDS danger period, of course let them keep it with them all night. To promote attachment

to the lovie, stroke their cheek with it while they nurse or put it into their hand, the one that usually grasps your hair (if it's long), the little fat roll under your breasts, your shirt edge. Have two identical ones and use them interchangeably: it's insurance against losing the beloved object. You can increase the chance of attachment by sleeping with the lovie tucked between your breasts for a week before you start, so it smells like your body (you'll have to leave it unwashed).

2. Have your baby clutch the lovie whenever they nurse or are likely to fall asleep (in a stroller, pack, or car seat. Give it to them whenever they go into the crib. Within two weeks, you should observe a "conditioned response:" soothing/getting sleepy when it's in their hand.

Some babies attach easily and intensely; others are lukewarm about it. If it's the former, the relationship will become a deep love and abiding friendship. Decide now whether you want your child toting it everywhere for the next five to twenty-five years, helping them feel secure wherever they go. If not, restrict the lovie to the crib or bed. There are arguments on both sides. Whichever way you go, do it with forethought and consistency.

3. Once your baby bonds with the lovie, start putting them in their crib awake. Stop nursing/feeding a minute or two early—before they fall asleep—and rouse them gently if they have drifted off. Add a short "Going to Sleep Routine" between feeding and going into the crib, e.g., sing a lullaby (always the same one), say goodnight to the moon or a favorite picture in the baby's room, kiss each cheek, and then swiftly put them into the crib with the lovie in hand.

Most babies will protest, especially if entrenched in falling asleep in arms, on the breast/bottle, or in a swing. Soothe them first with just words, then pat their tummy or jiggle them a bit and keep repeating the soothing words (in a reassuring but rather flat monotone). If all these steps fail, pick them up and rock them. After they calm a bit *(don't* let them fall asleep in your arms), start the routine over from the lullaby. Don't get discouraged or worried if you have to repeat these five to ten times the first night and it takes one-and-a-half to two hours. Every time you repeat it, the baby is learning. It typically takes up to five nights to training to succeed.

Once your "going to sleep routine" is set so that you can put the baby down in the crib and they fall asleep on their own (some fussing, say five minutes to ten not at top volume, is okay), it's time for Phase Two: Extending the Baby's Sleep Cycles.

1. First, work toward a four-hour sleep cycle. If less than four hours have passed since the last feeding, repeat the soothing (#3 above) to get the baby back to sleep without nursing or a bottle. This may take a few days of crying, too: keep steady!

2. Increase the increments by an hour every seven to ten days. Use your experience (e.g., your five-months-old baby can't stretch past six hours) and your intuition to judge if the baby does need feeding and try again a week later.

3. At seven months and fifteen pounds, almost all babies are ready for "The Big One: Sleeping through the Night." They can go from bedtime (7:00 PM–8:00 PM, though some babies are on an earlier cycle and ready to go to sleep for the night at 6:00 PM) to early morning (5:30 AM–6:30 AM) without feeding. Every time your baby wakes, repeat the "Going to Sleep Routine" instead of nursing/using the bottle.

Easier said than done! This is one of the hardest things to pull off and stay sane. Here are the three essential tips to make it work:

1. Write down (really! the written word is magic) your plan in detail and agree with your partner on when/how to implement it (e.g., not right before a huge deadline at work, family visit, travel, etc.). If you are a single parent, try to recruit family members, friends, or a hired babysitter to help you get through the first three nights.

2. Your baby will more easily accept the new regimen when the

breasts are not in sight or smell range, so the non-nursing parent should take on the bulk of the work. However, parents differ in their ability to tolerate the baby's crying, so be realistic: plan on taking turns based on who can handle what length "shift" (and don't assign any value-judgment to it!). Have a clock you can see in the dark: you'll aim for at least twenty minutes per shift; absent a clock, it will feel like two hours.

3. The parent in the room with the baby is in charge, 100 percent. If you're the one in the *other* room and can't tolerate the crying (and want so barge it and take over), put on noise-canceling earphones and listen to soothing (or loud!) music. And if the parent with the baby needs to bail before twenty minutes are up, so be it: no hard feelings!

4. Naps (a quick overview here: a separate chapter follows if you need more information): The routine for naps comes after you've established a consistent, working sleep routine at bedtime. During the training period described above, it's optimal if you can follow the same "putting down in the crib awake" regimen for naps. But I know it may be just too trying and/or exhausting to do this training several times a day (especially if you have help from a partner at night but are alone during the day). As a stopgap measure, you can ease up on the naps and allow your baby to fall asleep in a carrier, stroller, or car seat, as long as you avoid nursing them to sleep.

If you do decide to brave it at naptime too, have someone help you (family member, babysitter) and use room-darkening shades during naptime and any other device you use at bedtime, such as noise machine or music. Allow twenty to thirty minutes of crying when you put the baby down awake but not longer. If after three tries, your baby won't go to sleep, abort this mission and let her fall asleep in a carrier or stroller (inside your house/apartment is fine).

Too hard? No progress after a week of training? Get sleep coaching from a professional.

The 5:00 AM Wake-Up

Our seven-months-old baby has been a great sleeper (even gave up the middle of the night waking recently), but when Daylight Savings Time ended, she started waking up at 5 AM. We thought we'd wait it out to let her adjust to the new time and she'd go back to 6:00 AM (much more reasonable), but no such luck. We tried keeping her up later at night but other than a miserable time from 8:00 PM to 9:00 PM, we have seen no results. How can we explain to her that we are not farmers? Can we retrain her to wake up at a more suitable hour for modern urban living? I have never been SO TIRED in my life (even when I used to get up three times a night to nurse).

This is a common problem with infants; perhaps it's the hunter-gatherer genetic code. Sometimes it's triggered by a time change (or jet lag), but often it just appears as a baby transitions from nights punctuated by several wakings to feed to sleeping through the night. Delaying bedtime may help, but it takes five to seven days before it "takes," and, as in your case, often increases misery at night for no rewards in the morning.

Here is how you train your daughter to sleep in (before she is a teenager, when sleeping in will no longer be a problem at all!).

1. Record when she awakes for five days in a row. Pick the earliest time as your starting point. If she wakes at 5:15 AM, 5:00 AM, 5:05 AM, 5:20 AM, and 5:10 AM, then 5:00 AM is it (sorry…).

2. Put a clock radio in her room, set to play music at 5:00 AM. Within a minute after it turns on, come into her room, pick her up, and proceed as if this is a perfectly reasonable time to start the day. Turn on lights, feed and change her, and play

with her in your usual daytime room. She'll probably want a morning nap earlier than usual; don't worry about that.

3. Repeat the clock radio routine for five days. You are working to create a conditioned response, whereby as soon as the music comes on, she wakes up and expects you.

4. After about five days, she will be trained to wake up to the music.

5. Now comes the crucial, somewhat sneaky, part: start moving the clock forward by five-minute increments each morning (5:05 AM, 5:10 AM, 5:15 AM). Remember: once the music is on, come right in and pick her up. After ten to twelve days, you should be able to move her waking to 6:00 AM or very close to it.

There is a limit to this method—most parents I have worked with were able to move their baby's wake-up time by forty-five to sixty minutes. Don't imagine you could stretch your daughter's sleep to 8:00 AM, as lovely as that sounds.

Finally, I wonder if part of your intense fatigue is your own reaction to the change from daylight savings time. A lot of people don't realize they suffer from varying degrees of seasonal affective disorder (SAD): low energy, abnormal fatigue, and feeling down or full-blown depression, when the amount of sunlight they get each day suddenly drops by an hour. It often gets worse as the days get shorter but lifts in early spring. There are many high-intensity lamps available on the market (search for "SAD lamp"). Get a simple one for your dining table and sit close to it when you have your breakfast.

People vary a lot in how much light they need. I discovered about twenty-five years ago that I needed twenty minutes in the morning so that I don't feel like going to bed at 7:15 PM. Experiment to see how much you need. You should feel the difference very quickly: in one to three days. I hope you soon see your way to more sleep and more pep.

Daytime Naps

What's this I hear (and read) about three-months-old babies taking three naps a day at predictable times? What I would give for one nap at a predictable time lasting more than twenty minutes! My almost four-months-old baby falls asleep anywhere from four to seven times a day, but it's never at a set time. When she sleeps for thirty minutes, I count myself lucky. She may seem to be in a deep sleep in my arms, but when I transfer her to her crib, she awakes within a few minutes.

I realize it's partly because she was colicky for the first three months and we held her a lot and she often fell asleep in our arms, in a carrier, stroller, or on my chest when I couldn't stay upright anymore. But, well over a month later, she's a happy, bouncy baby, and I think she could and should take longer naps. How do I get her there?

You are right that most babies can—either on their own or with some training—begin a fairly regular nap routine and sustain longer naps by this age (for some lucky parents this happens much earlier). A rough schedule would be (with a lot of variations, of course):

- Wake up followed by one-and-a-half to two-and-a-half hours of active time and feeding
- 1–1.5 hours: morning nap
- 2–3 hours: active time and at least two feedings
- 1.5–2 hours: nap after lunch
- 2 hours: active time and feeding
- ½–1 hour: late afternoon nap
- 1.5–2 hours: active time and feeding
- Bedtime

The sequence will often start very early, between 5:00 AM and 6:00 AM (but read "The 5:00 AM Wake-Up" chapter on tips for nudging it closer to 6:00 AM), and results in an early bedtime, roughly twelve to thirteen hours after wake-up. Depending on your baby's inner clock and *your* family's schedules, it can start as late as 8:00 AM, with bedtime around 8:30 PM (allow for variations due to winter vs. summer sunlight as well). Figure out what would work best for you and aim to get there, still allowing for your baby's rhythms.

You did not mention her night-time sleep, so I'll assume that at night, you can put her down in her crib soothed and drowsy but not asleep, and she falls asleep on her own. She's probably waking at least once or twice to feed: that's fine for now.

Now, to the practical steps for training your baby to nap more regularly and for longer. You're right to realize the "sleep anywhere and anytime as long as it's not in the crib" is a key issue. You had to resort to holding, jiggling, carrying, and strolling because your baby had such a hard time soothing. But fortunately, as is the case for most (but not all) colicky babies her age, that's now over, and she's much more settled. So, the time is right for a nap intervention.

The *key* for both nighttime sleep and naps is to train your baby to fall asleep in the crib. The steps are described in detail in the "Getting your Baby to Sleep Through the Night" chapter. If you are starting from square one, focus on the training at the nightly bedtime first and leave the naptime for after you've established a solid routine of putting your baby in the crib awake. Doing it at naptime can be a bit more challenging since there's daylight and your baby may not be tired enough to be ready for her nap. Follow the same steps as the going-to-bed routine at night, adding the following:

1. Darken the room for naps with light-blocking shades.
2. Use the same words and songs (or music/sound machine) that you use at night.
3. Start with a set schedule and stick to it for at least a week. If you find that a given nap is always a big struggle, experiment first with pushing it to half an hour later. If that doesn't work, you needed to push it earlier: your baby was overtired, and therefore, she could not to soothe herself to sleep.

Think of the early afternoon nap (somewhere between 12:30 PM and 3:30 PM) as your *keystone*. Your goal is to get that nap to be the most predictable and longest. The other two naps (or three: some babies need four in all) can be moved and shortened—by trial and error—to support the afternoon nap. The first few days may be tough with the baby protesting intensely, so consider doing it when you have help: on the weekend with a partner or during the week with a babysitter or helpful family member. Take turns soothing the baby (follow the steps in the "going-to-sleep routine" at night). If the going is tough, it's alright to give yourself some slack and have one of the naps (preferably the last one) in a stroller while on a walk or just pushing it back and forth inside your home.

The late afternoon nap will eventually fall off by itself (in the next four to six months). However, if/when you notice that bedtime starts to move later because the baby is not tired enough, shave off the late afternoon nap to under twenty minutes. But consider whether the later bedtime is a benefit for you and your partner. Perhaps a parent gets home from work late and doesn't have enough time with the baby. It's easier to wake a baby from a twenty-, fifteen-, or even ten-minute nap and have a cheerful customer on hand than to wake them from an hour-long one. At twenty minutes, your baby is still in the light sleep portion of her sleep cycle. The same is true for (most) adults: a short nap is much more refreshing than a long, heavy one. Try it!

If your baby is in daycare, you'll only be dealing with the nap schedule over the weekend. Try to replicate the daycare's schedule, but don't get frustrated if it doesn't work nearly as well at home. Depending on how busy your weekends are and where you live, you may need to go with the flow: just to let your baby sleep in the stroller or car seat. There may be a period in your baby's development where scheduling your activities is best done around her afternoon nap (this applies to babies with a stay-at-home parent or nanny as well). Babies vary quite a bit in their nap flexibility: take your lead from yours.

During the week, you may be dealing with the late afternoon nap happening in a stroller, carrier, or car seat on the way home from daycare. That usually works well for both baby and parent: it makes transit easier, and the baby will often wake up on her own when you get home—hopefully not more than about twenty minutes since you left the daycare.

Finally, once you do get your baby on a fairly regular nap schedule, put yourself on a schedule too. Plan on a twenty-minute nap during her afternoon nap: it will make *you* much happier and more energetic. There is a lot of literature on the benefits of naps for adults, but I doubt you need much convincing.

Bedtime Battles: Toddlers (and Older)

Even if you had established a consistent routine in infancy and your toddler has been going to bed like a tired kitten, the day will most likely come when the system breaks down. It can start with an illness, a disruption in schedule, houseguests, Halloween, a scary experience, you name it. Sometimes it comes out of the blue: one day your child realizes that after they are in bed life goes on in the living room: maybe even a party! They begin to resist going to sleep, usually by having at least seventeen requests at bedtime, demanding that you stay with them, and popping out of bed and out of their room.

If your child has had a smooth "going-to-bed routine" as a baby, what you have on your hands is a limit-setting issue. If there had not been a routine in place, every day that passes will likely make the battles harder. Either way, jump in with both feet to create/re-establish a simple, brief, and totally consistent routine. For example:

1. After cleaning up (dinner dishes, toys), snuggle and read two or three short storybooks in the living room as a winding-down time.

2. Then move swiftly through tooth brushing and putting on pajamas to one or two storybooks in bed, a lullaby, goodnight kiss, and lights off (leave a nightlight on if your child is scared).

From here on, the most important thing is your child needs to know with absolute firmness that they have to stay in their bed. Don't tell them to "go to sleep," since you can't enforce that. Rather say, "You have to stay in your bed." You can help it along by letting them listen to a CD of simple stories or lullabies (the same one every night!). The lullabies should have songs with specific titles or opening lines (you'll see why in a minute). Often you need to start this training sitting next to your child's bed and enforcing the routine by turning the CD off the instant they try to get out of bed. Don't get excited! Monotone consistency will get the best results.

About those seventeen requests:

1. Ask your child what they need *before* getting into bed and fulfill these requests within reason.

2. Limit the requests to two within a small range of options (e.g., a sip of water, one trip to the toilet, a goodnight kiss from the "off-duty" parent). Stay firm!

You'll probably have to sit by your child's bed until they fall asleep (hopefully within twenty to thirty minutes). Don't worry—it's a temporary measure. Once they have internalized the rule and stay quietly in their bed, you can build up longer intervals when you are out of their room. A few minutes after the CD (or other music-producing gadgets: I'll use CD here for brevity) starts, tell them: "I have to check something. I'll be back on the Choo-Choo Train Song," which you know comes in thirty seconds (since you have the CD memorized by now). Add: "Lie quietly until I am back." If needed, call it out again from the hallway. It may take many repetitions to get this down. Be sure to praise your child for waiting quietly once she does.

When your child can wait quietly for thirty seconds, increase your time out of her room to sixty, then ninety seconds, again telling them precisely when you'll be back. Over ten days, build up by two-minute increments. Your goal is to stay in her room for the first two songs and return on the last one. She'll either fall asleep in the interim (assuming a thirty-minute CD) or will hold onto a thread of wakefulness to make sure you come back. Once you say, "I am back. Good night," she'll fall asleep in two seconds.

If your child is two years old or more and has a good grasp of cause and effect, help this along with a sticker chart in which you reward forward steps each morning. The stickers should culminate in a special outing or party to celebrate the new accomplishment: pleasant bedtime for everyone.

Pacifiers: Yea or Nay?

My three-months-old baby wants to suck all the time. After ten minutes on a side, she's full but wants to stay on the breast for another hour. I want to meet her needs, but I can't have her velcroed to me all day. We're considering a pacifier, but every time I see a four-year-old with one lodged in his mouth, I shudder. Your advice?

Pacifiers do generate passionate debates. I, too, cringe at kids cruising around town with pacifiers permanently implanted in their mouths, but I've never seen one go to college that way, so let's not panic. Pacifiers are useful for soothing babies, especially fussy ones, and getting them back to sleep in the middle of the night. But you will have a problem if your child grows extremely dependent on a pacifier and you don't gradually restrict its use and then wean her.

Decide about a pacifier based on these questions:

1. Is your baby very sensitive? Fussy? Wants to suck all the time?

2. Is your life hectic? Are both parents working? Are you stretched to the maximum?

3. Does an older child still require a lot of attention or an aging parent need your care?

4. Are you far from family? Have little help?

Have you answered "yes" to most of these? I advise trying a pacifier. Is it a crutch? Yes, of course, but raising a baby takes many hands and feet, so a crutch is probably exactly what you need. You can see if your baby will find her thumb or fingers. These never get lost but are, obviously, harder to wean from. Your baby may be finicky: try several pacifiers until you find one she likes (some babies never take to them).

If you go for a pacifier, bear in mind:

1. Pacifiers work well for helping babies back to sleep but often fall out/get lost in the crib. Attach the pacifier with a short ribbon (no more than two-inch) to the edge of your baby's sleeve and teach her to find it on her own in the middle of the night by moving her hand for her until she grabs it. Or put an extra pacifier in a box in the corner of the crib so you can find it in the dark. Eventually, your child can learn to get it from the box herself.

2. Be honest with yourself: it's really easy to overuse the pacifier! Don't resort to it every time your baby cries; develop other soothing methods.

3. With time, gradually increase restrictions on using the pacifier: first only at home, then only in her room, finally only in her crib/bed.

4. Around age three is a good time to wean from the pacifier. By now, the pacifier hopefully "lives" in your child's bed. Start with a discussion, lay out a step-by-step plan, and promise a big reward once she's "pacifier-free."

We did that with my son, taking advantage of his upcoming third birthday and his motivation to be a "big boy." His "pacifier habit" was one in the mouth, one in each hand. We began with the easier step—the hand-held ones. We put them to bed at night in a shoebox I made into "Pacie's Bed." That went well. Soon he started placing the mouth pacifier in the box too after a goodnight quick suck. The pacifiers spent the night right there, in the corner of his crib.

A little while later, we were driving across the country. In Illinois, my son wanted to fling the pacifier out the window. We explained we were driving fast and that, once he threw it out, it wasn't coming back. "See," I pointed to a tree, "we're next to it now, but in a minute, it'll be so far we won't see it." He turned back to watch the tree vanish, but still wanted to do it. We rolled down his window, and he tossed it, yelling, "Bye, Pacie!"

Minutes later, he wanted it back. He was sad. "Pacie is all alone by the side of the road!" "Yes," I said, "but just now a bunny rabbit hopping near the road found it and took it home." It worked! We continued with "Bunny and Pacifier Adventures" all the way home.

Weaning from Breast and/or Bottle

My baby is eighteen months, and I'm ready to wean her before she turns two, first from breastfeeding, and soon thereafter from the bottle. She eats a wide array of foods and drinks from a sippy cup (we have several different types, and she likes them all), so she doesn't need the nursing and bottle for nutrition. She is, however, clearly very fond of both and uses them for comforting. Truth be told, I rely on them too: to soothe crying spells, calm her down after tantrums, and get her to mellow out in preparation for bedtime. So, given the emotional attachment to nursing and the bottle, I am wondering how to wean her in a way that won't be too hard (for her AND me), let along harmful.

You are spot-on in realizing your daughter's need for the breast and bottle is emotional, not nutritional. This is a good place to start: make sure that you offer plenty of liquids for her to drink. Water is your first choice for hydration and milk for nutrition (whether animal or plant source, depending on your pediatrician's recommendations and issues with lactose tolerance). Still, variety has a place too, so fruit juice with no added sugar, and diluted if too sweet, will keep her interest in drinking.

Now to the core of the issue: the emotional attachments to breast and bottle. First, ask yourself honestly if you are ready to wean because YOU want to, or if you are feeling pressure from the outside.

If it's pressure, whether from other parents, books, the internet, or elsewhere, my advice is to ignore it. It's up to you! Once you've nursed your baby for six to eight months (assuming you wanted to and you were successful—not everyone is), you've provided most of the health benefits of nursing. If your life circumstances make breastfeeding burdensome, ease up on yourself. Having more time to rest, take care of things you need to do, and occasionally pamper yourself "at the expense" of breastfeeding will have great benefits for you, your baby, and your whole family.

If you're not ready to give up nursing altogether, you can limit it to once or twice a day (e.g., after waking in the morning and before bedtime). However, be aware that the milk supply will dwindle and may be uneven, so your baby may lose interest. That said, many toddlers and preschoolers can happily nurse only once or twice a day, and it becomes a precious time of closeness and comforting. If you want to go this route and avoid battles about it in the middle of the day, the nursing needs to take place in her room, with shades drawn and either silence or very soft music/sound machine. Give the nursing a name and be clear that "nursey-nurse" only happens at those set times. Most kids will go along with this structure fairly easily. If you're having a lot of struggles with your child asking/demanding to nurse repeatedly at other times (when you don't want to), you are probably better off cutting it out altogether.

Weaning from breast or bottle presents an opportunity for mastery and a big achievement for your child, rather than a loss. If you decide to wean "cold turkey," you have all the power, and your child feels powerless (and may, of course, protest intensely) and experience it as a loss. To make it her achievement, it has to be gradual, discussed, and taken on together. Break the process down into stages and talk your child through each one. Making a poster with illustrations helps, too, especially if there is room for gold stars for each day of success at a given stage.

Here's an example with bottle weaning:

Stage 1: Start with limiting the bottle to three times a day: depending on your child and your daily schedule, it could be upon waking in the morning, after a nap, and before bedtime. Or, if you have to get out of the house swiftly in the morning, make it work for you by having your child get a bottle only in the stroller going to daycare and back, plus before bed.

Stage 2: The bottle lives in the child's crib and room. She can have it at those three times mentioned in Stage 1 but only in her room. When she's ready to get up and out of her room to play, the bottle gets left behind.

Stage 3: Now limit the bottle to only once a day. Your child can choose the time, though you might encourage it as being just before bedtime—that's when you're getting your maximum benefit from the soothing it provides.

Meanwhile, as you start the process, build with your child a repertoire of alternatives for soothing when she is upset, tired, or cranky. A favorite stuffed animal, a pacifier, or a special comfy pillow are all good substitutes. Adding words such as "This is your 'feel better bear'" helps create a strong association.

Stage 4: Plan a "mission accomplished" ritual with your child: "When you're all done with bottles [or done with nursing from mommy's breast], we will celebrate with ___." Fill in the blank with an idea for a party, a special gift, or a "Bye-bye Bottle" celebration. This celebration could include putting all the old bottles in a box and sending them to "Bottle Land;" actually shipping the box to some address (your office?), putting it in a Salvation Army donation box, etc. Be creative, but avoid putting it in the garbage. "Bottle Land" can feature in a story you make up together with your child. Make it into a small book with illustrations based on your child's imagination.

If you are weaning from breastfeeding, these stages still apply, except for sending your breasts away. Instead, have a little, "Bye-bye Breasts" celebration with an announcement: "From now on, Mommy's breasts stay inside her shirt, and they won't have any milk in them anymore." Explain to your child in straightforward terms that your body is all done making milk because she doesn't need it anymore to make her grow. She has all the things she likes to eat and drink for becoming bigger and stronger. To help this transition along, introduce a new food she can now have instead: it could be sorbet or ice cream, a special cookie, or a new, particularly tasty fruit.

Stranger Anxiety and Separation Difficulties

Oh, my, this is embarrassing! My nine-month-old baby has started howling whenever my mother-in-law comes over to visit or babysit. My parents live out of town, so I can't, in good conscience, tell her it's the same when my mom comes. This means I can't leave the baby with Grandma (unless I'm willing to put up with two miserable human beings), and now I'm worried about the babysitter we're hoping to hire soon (we've already started interviewing).

It's a problem with other people as well. If we're at the store and someone leans over to say how cute she is (she is!), she starts crying, but I don't worry about their feelings too much. This is a baby who used to love attention from anyone: cashiers, bus drivers, passersby, you name it. Is this going to go away by itself, or should I be doing something about it?

Your baby is right on the mark developmentally, so three cheers for her, despite the embarrassment and inconvenience. Around seven to nine months, many (but not all) babies develop "stranger anxiety." They'll cry, turn away, even flail their arms if anyone other than the parents (and a babysitter or nanny if they are there daily) come near. It's an important milestone: your baby has learned to distinguish you, parents and primary caretakers, from the rest of the world. Other adults with smiles and open arms who, in the first months of life, were perfectly acceptable to hold and soothe her are now taboo: they are clearly not Mommy or Daddy.

What can you do about the wailing? Not much, unless your

mother-in-law is willing to come every day and get the baby accustomed to her face. Otherwise, your choices are to wait it out or put up with the crying. Typically, it lasts only a couple of months, and the crying subsides very quickly when you disappear from view. Without you in the room, a substitute will usually be accepted quickly, unless your baby has moved on from stranger anxiety to separation anxiety as, eventually, most babies will.

How's separation anxiety different? It's a more advanced level of cognitive development: it marks the moment when your child realizes that when *she* doesn't see you, *you* don't exist (as far as she's concerned). The reaction you see in this case—whimpering, crying, or shrieking—is your child's distress about your disappearance. You'll first see it at home when you go out of the room for a moment. This is where Peek-A-Boo comes in: playing it teaches your child that you disappear and then come right back. Integrating this information into a certainty that you are still around, even when she doesn't see you, takes a while. A parallel, usually earlier process (starting at about four months) happens with objects, and it can call for similar games. You can hide a block inside a basket or under a pillow while saying, "Where is it?" and then reveal it with, "There it is!" This fosters the development of what Jean Piaget called "object permanence:" a child's realization that objects continue to exist even when they don't see them (that's huge!).

These three developmental processes often happen in sequence (object permanence first, stranger anxiety next, then separation anxiety), but they often overlap as well. Separation anxiety lasts the longest and can be the most challenging. With regular routines, most kids adjust to your leave-taking, be it every morning from home or at preschool or daycare, or when you go out at night, before age two. But not all do. And even a kid who's been fine with separation for a long time can suddenly start having a tough time with it. Sometimes you can figure out why: something scary or disruptive has happened, or you were gone for a few days on a work trip. But often you can't put your finger on the trigger—it seems to happen out of the blue.

In general, what helps kids deal with separations most effectively is predictability and a very simple, brief, and consistent (exactly the same every day!) leave-taking routine. For example, if you go out for dinner once a week, try to have the babysitter always (or, at least, most of the time) come at a set time (say, right after your child's dinner) and have the same repertoire of activities with your child. Meanwhile, you say your goodbye in the same non-dramatic, fairly swift manner every time. Depending on your child's age, you can remind them that you'll be back when they're asleep and check on them and that they'll see you in the morning. You can put something small (a leaf, a colorful napkin from your dinner) in their crib/bed/ under their pillow so that they'll find it in the morning: it will show them that you came back, as promised, while they were sleeping.

If you take your child to daycare and they have a hard time when you leave, have a short sequence for your arrival, getting them settled, and saying goodbye (see more details in the chapter: "Starting Preschool and Separation Troubles"). Leave promptly even if they cry and ask the teachers to text you an update (photo of them smiling is best) about twenty minutes after you've gone.

If the separation difficulties persist for several weeks and your routine (in consultation with the preschool staff) does not ease things, you should consult with a child development specialist or therapist.

Attachment Parenting

We are expecting our first baby soon and feel bombarded by different approaches to parenting. With the Time *Magazine cover "Are You Mom Enough?" versus the buzz around the detached adult-centered French parenting of Bringing up Bébé (we do know we are not signing up for the "Tiger Mother" approach). We are in a tailspin. Is there a middle road?*

Let's begin with the *Time* magazine cover from May 2012: indeed, a very provocative photograph. A very mature-looking three-year-old boy, wearing (to add confusion to the mix) "masculine" army fatigue-style pants stands on a stool to reach the breast of his lithe, overly skinny (another issue...) mom in skintight pants and top. He nurses, looking at the camera with an ambiguous expression.

Is he saying "In your face!" or "Hope this doesn't get on my Facebook page in five years"?

First, I find the shameless exploitation of a mother's natural anxiety about being "good enough" with the title "Are You Mom Enough?" appalling. Second, the cover belies the sensible, balanced story that also does justice to the ideas that predate the current buzz by over twenty years ("the continuum concept," the "family bed," etc.) The cover provoked an avalanche of responses in the media. At the risk of pouring a teaspoon into the ocean, here's my view.

Surely much good comes for baby and parents (especially mothers) from attachment parenting's "trinity" (Are you surprised to learn that its "prophets," Dr. William and Martha Sears, are devout Catholics?): 1. devoted, often exclusive breastfeeding 2. co-sleeping and 3. carrying ("baby-wearing"). But the extremes advocated by many practitioners worry me for the children's development and the parents' sanity. What do I consider extreme? Here are examples:

1. Nursing so often your baby is essentially latched onto the breast day and night
2. Never letting a baby cry beyond the first whimper
3. Getting no uninterrupted sleep for three or more years
4. Never leaving your baby with anyone (not even grandparents)
5. Never going out without your children
6. Not putting your child down for long enough that she can experiment with and learn how to entertain herself
7. Nursing a four-year-old in public (cover of *Time* Magazine included).

So. what do I recommend instead? Let me illustrate what I consider the "middle road:"

1. I do support breastfeeding nearly exclusively in the first months

of life if you can (do read Emily Oster's *Cribsheet* chapter on breastfeeding for a sane and practical approach). But I advise new parents to start acquainting their infant with a bottle around four weeks so the nursing mother can get some breaks. The most valuable times a nursing mother can substitute a bottle for breastfeeding are the very first nighttime feeding so she can sleep through that, or an afternoon for a nap or short outing.

2. I encourage parents to introduce on or two trusted caretakers by three or four months so they can have a few "dates" each month for exclusive couple time. Accustoming a baby to a sitter at that age is usually fairly easy. Around eight months, when many babies go through developmentally appropriate "stranger anxiety," or when they are even older, it can prove much harder.

3. Co-sleeping works well for some families (though I am obliged to note the Academy of Pediatrics' continued opposition to bed-sharing because of the risk of the baby suffocating). But, most parents I have talked to—hundreds of them—can't get the sleep they need to function sanely and competently the next day with a baby or toddler squirming in their bed (true for many a stay-at-home parent too). New parents manage without much sleep for the first few months, but sleep deprivation takes its toll. Most parents will give almost anything for six hours of uninterrupted sleep. Admittedly, teaching your baby to sleep on their own can be hard, so I offer a long chapter on that.

The bottom line is: do attach strongly and deeply to your baby, but don't become superglued. Keep a balance between devoted parenting and continuing your adult life. Trust your instincts and, on occasion, even listen to your mom!

II. Behavior, Play, and Social Skills

Sharing and Taking Turns: First Steps

My one-year-old is about to start a toddler playgroup/part-time daycare (three mornings a week), and I realize from observing him interacting with other kids when we're with friends that he might be a bit of a menace in the playroom. He has no siblings at home, so he's never had to share anything with anyone. I don't want him starting on the wrong foot, grabbing toys from all the other kids (he's a swift one, and strong!). Can I start teaching him to share now?

You are right on the mark! It is absolutely not too early to teach the basic building blocks of sharing, as long as you realize this is a long game, and don't expect immediate results. You build the foundation of sharing and taking turns (taking turns, after all, is a form of sharing) in gradual phases based on your child's motor and cognitive skill development first, and, a bit later, considering their emotional maturation as well. Here are the steps, ordered chronologically, starting as early as six months (though seven or eight months is just fine):

1. Start with a very simple game: give your baby a rattle or small toy he can easily grab and say, "For you!" or "Here you go!" When the baby grabs it, smile, applaud, and encourage him.

2. Next, open your hand, put it close to his, and say, "Thank you!" As soon as he releases the toy, take it and say, "Thank you!" again. Now repeat with you giving it to him. Play this as long as you can hold his attention: it could be anywhere for three repetitions to a dozen. The more repetitions, the faster he learns. Be forewarned that you might tire of it long before he does.

3. Once he's mastered that, the two of you are ready to move on. Pick two identical (or very similar) objects, such as two red blocks or two small blue balls. Sit across from each other (making a diamond-shaped "playing field" between your legs and your child's legs; feet touching adds to the fun and his focus on the game). Announce, "Trade!" and exchange your red block for his. Next, do it with the balls: on saying "Trade," roll your ball toward him and ask for his. He might want to hold onto both balls for a bit—that's fine. Just wait until he's ready to relinquish one of them so you can go back to playing "Trade."

4. Now you're ready to graduate to "Your Turn; My Turn," with only one toy (pick something a bit more attractive than those plain blocks). Give the toy to your child and say, "Your turn!" Wait a few seconds, put out your hand, and say, "My turn." When he gives you the toy, say, "Thank you!" Hold it very briefly and give it back, saying, "Your turn." Play this and encourage your child to take over announcing whose turn it is. Switch between steps two and three until your child has it down and seems to be getting bored with these games. When that happens, he is ready to move to the next level.

5. Play the trading game with toys that are *not identical,* e.g., trading a toy car for a small stuffed animal, blocks for a train

engine, a doll for a xylophone. Be creative, try to anticipate which items your child will want more, and have him trade you more small toys he doesn't want for something bigger he covets. This game works best if you sit facing each other with each of you holding a basket with several items in it. Start with four or five items and gradually make it more complex with a larger number of toys and trading things that are more and more unlike each other. You can add words here, such as "I see you really want this big dinosaur, so trade me three small toy animals for it."

6. Continue the "Taking Turns" game a well, adding a way to mark how long each of you has the toy. Start with just counting to three, then five, and then ten. Later on, when your child is at least eighteen months, start making it more abstract with "two minutes," remembering, however, that actual time and minutes (let alone hours) don't sink in until after age four.

Many parents favor using a timer, but that's still very abstract. *You* have a feel for how long three minutes take to pass, but to your child, the timer just mysteriously dings at some point. Something that shows progress they can see, such as a large hourglass sand timer (they still exist!) or an analog clock with a prominent seconds hand, is much better. A better way to help your child have a sense of time passing and how long "two minutes" or "five minutes" take is to mark it with a song. Put on a two-minute song and tell your child "When the song is done it will be two minutes, and the end of your turn" (this is a very helpful technique for many other situations such as, "We'll start getting ready for bed in five minutes").

After your child gets good at each of these steps, it's time to practice them with other kids. Start, if possible, with an older child who can understand your explanation that "we are teaching Rebecca to take turns," and play along. Be sure to show appreciation for both kids for sharing or trading, but keep it simple and specific: "I can see how well you are taking turns" (overdoing praise is a common pitfall). Undoubtedly, sharing and taking turns is a keystone in your child's development and ability to function with his peers. It takes a lot of practice, as I am sure you know from observing not just kids on the playground, but probably also some adults in your life.

Aggression: Hitting, Biting, Shoving and More

My until-now-sweet-as-pie eighteen-months-old boy has had his even-keeled, outgoing personality suddenly hijacked by some mysterious force. At the preschool (he started three months ago), he now grabs toys from other kids, shoves them, hits and—to my horror— has even bitten both a child and a teacher. At home, he's "king of the roost," so he's not been aggressive, but we are expecting another baby in a few months, and I am already worried sick about their safety. How can I turn this around?

Dealing with aggression is one of the hardest tasks for parents, and it's often more so when your child is the aggressive one. Not that being the recipient is much fun, especially when it comes to biting, but comforting a "victim" is easier than stopping an "attacker."

First: it's the job of the adults (parents at home and teachers at daycare/school) to protect children from being hurt and stop kids from hurting others (people or animals). Start by setting the clear limit: "No biting" or "No hitting." Don't get into lengthy explanations as to why: your young child loses focus after one sentence (see the chapter "Parentsplaining"). A long explanation muddles the message.

Next, if your child is overwhelmed by anger or frustration, offer an alternative target for the aggression, such as a biting ring for biters, pillow or punch bag for hitters, big yoga ball for kickers, or a large cardboard box for a kid who favors shoving. Tell your child those things don't feel pain, so it's okay to hit or kick them (but do say some things can break, especially things are precious to you. To be on the safe side, put those out of reach for a while).

On the Spot: When a child is aggressive, intervene as quickly as you can: remove your child from the child they've hurt and say firmly: "No hitting!" or "No biting!" If there is a second adult in the room (at preschool, playground, or home), divide the territory: one comforts the recipient (I don't like the word "victim"), and the other handles the aggressive child. Remember that the child who hit, bit, or kicked needs emotional support as much as the child who's been hurt. It's particularly important to help the aggressor (once simmered down) think of how to make the friend they've hit feel better. Ask your child: "What can you do to help Lucy feel better?" Suggestions may include bringing her a cold pack, Band-Aid, or stuffed animals to hug. It's valuable to model saying you're sorry, but don't put too much stock in it just repeating the words. It takes a lot of maturity to sincerely apologize (some adults I know are not quite there yet…).

The Aftermath: When your child has simmered down a bit, help her put the situation into simple words: "You wanted Jon's toy, but you can't hit him and take it. You have to ask." Go over the scenario and ask, "What can you do next time?" Give ample hugs and reassurance that sometimes it's very hard not to get mad or to hit, etc., but you (and the teachers) are there to help. Go over it by reading stories, or, better yet, making a small book with six to ten pages about "When I Get Mad." Draw or paste in pictures (download from the internet) of angry kids, plus hands, feet, and teeth for a page where you write: "Hands are for hugging, building block towers, teeth are for chewing and brushing, feet are for walking, kicking a ball…" You get the idea.

Sharing

Fighting over toys is the most common starting point for aggression, at home (with siblings or playdates) or daycare/preschool. Sharing is something your child learns in small steps. You can help this process along by modeling through play the simple building blocks of sharing: trading, asking for something you want, and taking turns.

Here's a brief overview (or go back to the prior chapter). Start by playing this game at home: sit facing each other, each with a pile of identical blocks. Say "Trade" and swap one block with each other. Repeat over and over, saying "Thank you" when you receive and "For you!" when you give. Repetition may bore you, but it's the key way young children learn. Your child sees that she can get something she wants from you by giving you something she has. Next, play a similar game of "Your turn-My turn," exchanging one item back and forth. As you play, you're fostering language development related to thinking and articulating "I want X" and asking for it. Adding "the magic word"—please—inculcates basic politeness, an important life skill.

If yours is the kind of child who is "always on the go and into everything," this will be more challenging and take longer. P-a-t-i-e-n-c-e is paramount, along with close supervision during playtime and a very structured day, both at daycare or preschool and at home.

Biting

Biting often appears around the same time that your child's potential situations of conflict increase (daycare, playdates). While it might be an aggressive act, there is also simply an ache in the gums that wants to be soothed by biting. If that seems to be going on, give your child a biting ring (hook it onto their pants or keep it in the fanny pack they wear during the day). Whenever you see a situation that might escalate into biting, try to jump in and redirect your child, saying, "Here, bite this ring, not your friend."

Of all young kids' aggressive behaviors, biting gets us adults most distraught because it is so primitive, so painful, and so risky: if the skin is broken, there is a chance of infection. If biting persists beyond a few isolated incidents, you need to work closely with the daycare or preschool on an intensive intervention plan. If it's happening when you are supervising, either at home or in the playground, you need to back off from playdates and busy playgrounds and give your child more time to develop emotionally. They *will* grow out of it.

Modeling

Finally, and perhaps more importantly, parents are the models for their children, so stick to your rules that you set for your child (and yourself!). Demonstrate by your behavior that anger is a real part of life and that we find ways to express it without aggression. *Never hit your child!* The idea that you can hit (or, God forbid, bite) a child to "show him how it feels" or discipline him *without* being angry is bogus. Hitting sends only one message to your child: *I am stronger, so it's okay for me to hit you.* When *you* are angry, model saying, "I am mad right now. I need to calm down." Demonstrate how you do it by closing your eyes and counting to ten, making a drawing, crumpling up old newspapers and stuffing them in a paper bag, or listening to soothing music.

If you find that too often you, yourself, are explosive or cannot stick to the rules, you need outside help beyond these tips. That help can come from a spouse, a supportive friend, or a preschool teacher. When that is not enough, work with a behavioral therapist, parenting coach, or family therapist.

When "Parentsplaining" Gets in the Way

I try to explain the rules to my two-year-old son whenever I have to lower the boom and set limits. For example, when I tell him to clean up his toys, I explain that everyone needs to put their things back where they belong so we can find them later, that we like a clean, tidy house and that, if he leaves a toy in the middle of the room, someone might trip on it and fall and get hurt. I guess I may be overcompensating for the way I remember being brought up: ordered to do things "because I said so," since I can't say that it's working. He looks at me when I explain things but still doesn't do what he's supposed to do (or stop what isn't supposed to do).

I am afraid you've fallen into a very common pitfall which I see parents stuck in much more these days than in the past: over-explaining. Of course, as a parent, you want your child to understand why you have the rules you do: you are ensuring their safety, the safety of others, good manners, and considerate behavior. But at age two, he's not ready for the complex process of listening, understanding, internalizing, and self-control. Your explanations not only go over his head, they actually undermine his understanding that this is a clear "No!" or definite instruction to do X or Y.

A good general rule is not to use more than double the number of words of your child's age. For example, with your two-year-old: "We don't hit [/kick/throw] things!" Or "Hold my hand now," when you're about to cross the street. With a three-year-old, you could add, "No! We don't hit! It hurts," or "Please put your toys away now."

I've noticed many parents phrase instructions as a question instead of a clear command. Thus, "It's time to put on your PJs, okay?" or "Don't push the coffee table, okay?" I guess we all want to be nice—nothing wrong with that. But it's confusing to young kids. They need to know you are telling them to do something, not asking them if they feel like doing it. Of course, be thoughtful about when you're giving "orders" versus when you are offering options. Certainly, there should be plenty of activities which your child can choose to do or not. But think through which ones those are and which are mandatory.

Within those mandatory activities, especially the going-to-bed routine, there can still be choices: the PJs with dogs or with flowers? Brush teeth and *then* read two books or the reverse order? Take the bear or the elephant—or both—to bed with you?

I don't mean to knock explanation completely. Surely, as your child develops emotionally and intellectually, you want him to understand how the world works, why we make rules, and what is socially acceptable behavior. But these explanations are best given not in the moment in which you are setting limits or requiring cooperation. Rather, save them for later and offer them within a conversation, such as, "Remember when we walked home and I said you had to hold my hand to cross the street? Why do you think I did?"

Better yet, get your child to explain the rule through role-playing, where he is the daddy, and you or one of his dolls or stuffed animals are the child, or playing school, reading books and asking about the rules in the story.

By the time your child is age five, I encourage you to begin to introduce more nuance by having family discussions about the rules and allowing your child to negotiate some amendments and modifications. Use the process to show him how the family's rules keep the system running smoothly. If he wants a rule relaxed or changed, ask him to balance that by taking a step up on the ladder of responsibilities to the family. For example, if he wants to have more time to watch a favorite TV show, he needs to put in more time helping with household chores. So yes, he can watch for another 15 minutes, but only after he helps bring the dinner dishes to the kitchen.

Getting these steps down now will set up a foundation for how you negotiate rules and responsibilities when things get much more challenging—in the teenage years.

Swearing Toddlers

Recently our son has started saying, "Oh, shit" when he gets mad. We don't curse at home, so he must be getting it at preschool. We've been ignoring it to avoid encouraging him to say it (though it is pretty funny!). Should we do more?

Your son is quite advanced in verbal skills and deciphering social cues and norms. He gets that this word has more power than the usual, "Oh, no." Your reaction will determine if this is a passing phase or his favorite sport. Ignoring it much of the time, as you have been doing, is a good approach, but you also want to "catch it" as an opportunity to teach about manners and acceptable ways to express anger and frustration.

Manners

Say: "We don't use the word 'shit' because it's not polite." Ask him if he knows what it means. If he does, say: "So you can see why people don't like it if you say 'poop' to them when you are mad. You wouldn't like someone to say that to you, would you?"

You should probably explain "polite" a little more, e.g., "Polite means saying 'Please' and 'Thank you,' eating with your fork and spoon, and waiting your turn. We like that!" Ask him for his own examples of being polite, both at home and preschool. Make a poster of "Polite Things to Say and Do" to hang up where he can show it off.

Anger

Honestly, this is much more important. Most adults I know wish they had mastered more acceptable and productive ways of expressing anger and frustration as kids, or at least by now.

Here are five simple steps:

1. Make a list together of what makes him angry. Share a couple of things (toned down to his level) that make you angry—some for which there is no one to blame (rain on Sunday) and others where there is (preferably not him).

2. Now ask him how he feels when he is angry. This can be very hard for him to put into words. Have him show you with his face and his body. Make a list with simple drawings and/or cut out photos from magazines (or print from the internet) to illustrate (angry faces, punching fists).

3. Now make a list of words and actions for expressing frustration and anger using drawings or photos of him making angry faces. One column for acceptable actions and another for those you won't countenance.

4. Together, come up with a list of words that are acceptable to you. Of course, "I am furious" would be accurate, but you want words with more pizzazz and power. Try a Yiddish expression such as *Oy, Gevalt!* He will love having his special words, and you would be justified in finding it amusing. Some other good ones (none involving body parts or curses): *Oy vey! Vey is mir! Gey aveck* [go away]! I am *ufgekocht* [furious]!

5. Also, check with the preschool director, in the most non-

accusing way you can muster, how the teachers are expected to react. If it's more or less in line with your policy (and these suggestions), let the director know you agree and appreciate the approach. If there is a wide gap, you need a serious conversation to better align responses at home and school.

It's vital to address what actions are okay when your son is in a rage. Your rule should be (in so many words): "No hurting people (including himself—some kids bite or hit themselves in frustration or rage) and no breaking things." Options are:

1. Tearing up old newspapers and/or crumpling them into tight balls and throwing the paper balls at the wall (provided he'll pick up later when he has calmed down, with your help).

2. Stomping on a partially deflated ball or a thick plastic bag full of old crackers (good sound effects. Make sure the bag is well sealed).

3. Hitting/stomping/jumping on a bop bag.

Finally—and obviously—model, model, model. Let him see you get frustrated and angry (less often and less intensely than him) while still keeping your head and minding your language. Wait thirty years, and you've got it made!

Food Fights

I never thought I'd come to this: I hear my mother's voice in my ear as I say to my daughter, "Just one more bite!" Argh... I still remember how I hated the cajoling, threatening (no dessert, ever!), and deal-making. I grew up believing I was a picky eater and, as an adolescent and young woman, struggling with weight and diets. I swore I wouldn't do that to my kids, but here I am. I can't seem to bear seeing my child sit in front of her plate and not even be willing to take one bite. I try to cook things she likes, but her list of acceptable food is down to mac and cheese and blackberries (go figure!), and that does not constitute a healthy diet.

I know my attempts to bargain and pressure her are not working, but I don't know what else to do.

How right you are! What you are doing not only doesn't work but, as you can testify from your own childhood, is doing damage that can last years. I hate telling parents that I think what they are doing is damaging. It's excruciating to hear and belies the fact that they're doing the best they know how. In this case, it's not "the best" you aspire to, but it is familiar and comes naturally from the sometimes not fully conscious repertoire of what you heard at home.

Let's start with three basic facts (assuming your daughter's weight is within the normal range for her age and height, and her overall health is fine):

- Palates vary a great deal between people and are gradually shaped by the culinary culture in which we live. So just because your child doesn't like anything with a strong flavor now doesn't mean she'll never acquire a taste for it; witness kindergarteners in France gobbling up very ripe brie served as part of the school lunch.
- You really can't make her eat. You can make her sit at the table with the family for meals and require she eat given foods or amounts if she wants dessert or other treats (though I really would not condition other activities on food).
- Left to her own devices, she will eat when she's hungry.

So please stop the pressure, bargaining, and whatever else you are doing. Instead, set meals up this way:

1. She is expected to sit at the table with the family for at least five minutes at ages two to three and ten minutes from age four on.
2. You serve whatever food the family generally eats.
3. You can make a rule that she has to take one bite from the food on offer if she's never tasted it before. This should hold for three to four times that food is served because it may take that long for a child to get accustomed to a flavor (or

texture) and decide whether she likes it or not. If, after that, she insists she doesn't like it, drop it.

4. If she doesn't want to eat any of the food you serve, she can get a container from the fridge that had mac and cheese and one vegetable, such as carrots sticks or snap peas (those are the most popular with young kids). That's her meal. Don't bother heating it up, and make no fuss about it. The next week, substitute another option (if she'll eat it) such as peanut butter and jam sandwich, crackers and cheese, apple slices, but make it a minimalist spread.

5. No desserts except fresh fruit.

6. Keep your lips sealed: make no comments—neither negative *nor positive*—about what she's eaten. With your partner and, if you have them, other kids, exchange pleasant remarks about how the dish tastes (specific are better than general praise, so "this casserole tastes like roasted chicken" instead of "this is so delicious!"). *Don't* overdo it: she'll catch on that it's a show meant to influence her.

7. After her allotted stay at the dinner table, she may ask to leave. Let her do that, unless she wants to stay to participate in the conversation (make it reasonably interesting for her).

8. If soon after a meal had ended, she is hungry, she may get her container of food from the fridge and sit at the table (by herself) and eat as much as she wants. Again, make no comments, though it's ever so tempting to say, "You see, you were hungry! If you'd eaten more at dinner..." You know how it goes.

9. Plan on going out two or three times a month (if you can afford the time and cost) to restaurants that serve simple meals quickly. Don't restrict what she may order (even if it's always pizza or French fries).

10. Let her play with her food. She can make sculptures out of vegetables, decorate a plate with fruit slices (check out

the *Play with Your Food* book series), or play "shopping at the grocery store" with either plastic or real food.

Do all of that and practice a little mantra you recite to yourself before each meal, something like "She's eating to feed *her* body, not *my* soul," or more simply "No comments, mom!" And try to enjoy your meal!

Clean-up Time

My twenty-months-old loves to strew his toys all around the living room. He can occupy himself for up to half an hour just taking things out of baskets, spreading them around, lining them up, and then scattering them. He also loves to build towers and then smash them down, dispatching blocks or Duplo pieces to every corner of the room. I know that's how he plays, and right now, it's convenient that he occupies himself this way and too hard to get him to focus on following my instructions, so I just leave the mess until after his bedtime and then pick everything up. But I want to get him in the habit of cleaning up. Is it too soon? How can I get him to cooperate without being too harsh?

You are right that scattering toys, knocking down towers, and the like is part of a toddler's "play menu." But cleaning up can be too, and will not only reduce your work (though not significantly, at least initially) but instill good habits of responsibility and cooperation.

When they're under age two, you can't count much on their either wanting to please you (on the contrary, the "Terrible Twos" are the quintessential time to oppose you) or rewards when a task is completed. Instead, at this age you should focus on two simple elements:

1. Predictable routine
2. Making clean-up a game

Let's start with a predictable routine. So much of what goes on in the world surrounding your toddler is, from his point of view, surprising and incomprehensible. The simplest things we take for granted are still big discoveries for him. Anything that he can begin to anticipate and "know the drill" about gives him a sense of mastery and security. Thus, clean-up time needs to happen every day, at about the same time. I would suggest the following:

1. If your child is home with you most of the day, clean up mid-morning before a snack, mid-day before naptime, and evenings before bedtime. Even if, by chance, there's not much to clean up, you should still have clean-up time. I recommend making up a little clean-up-time jingle and singing it each time as you start.

2. If your child is in daycare (group or nanny-share), find out about clean-up time there and more or less copy their procedure (if they have a jingle, adopt it) at home. You'll need to do it only once on weekdays, but weekends and holidays will let you do it several times a day and reinforce it at home.

3. Now make it engaging for your child: Don't overdo explanations about why it's important to clean up: they just confuse your child. All he needs to know is that it's clean-up time and that we put the toys back on shelves, in baskets, and so on. Of course, for an older child (three and up), a simple explanation about safety and the pleasures of tidiness is a valuable addition.

4. Make clean-up an interesting game or challenging task. For example: start by saying, "Find all the red pieces and put them in the basket." Then continue with different colors, shapes, sizes, and so on. As your child develops, expand this to more sophisticated categories, e.g., "Find all the things you would see on a farm, at the grocery store, at a playground." You get the idea: tailor the level of categories to your child's cognitive development.

5. Occasionally (don't overdo it), you can motivate your child by first taking turns (I put in one block; you put in one block) and then having a race: who can put the most pieces in the box? Or who can clean up their side of the room fastest?

6. Make sure to have a desirable activity right after the clean-up, rather than the oft-resisted bedtime. In the evening or before naps, this should be a quiet activity: reading books, quietly coloring, cuddling with a bottle or sippy cup, or a song and finger-play.

And consider this: from what I have seen in the homes of most young kids, it's quite likely that your child has way too many toys available at any given time. This leads to boredom with many of them and increased scattering. I suggest you organize your child's toys in baskets or crates and bring out only a few at a time, keeping the others in a closet. So, for example, for a two-year-old, I would have two crates out at a time and rotate them every two days. For a three-year-old, three or four baskets switched every three days. Once your child reaches the age of five (some already at age four), he can manage his toys more independently and will enjoy arranging and rearranging them on the shelves.

And if a sibling is crawling, scooting, walking and grabbing their toys, have a couple of shelves of shared toys, but let the older child have his own shelves that the little one can't reach. He can put the toys he doesn't want to share on those.

Screen Time

I know, I know. . . the recommendation is to avoid exposing kids under age two to screens altogether, but reality trumps my best intentions. When I'm nursing my newborn and my almost-two-year-old is bouncing off the walls, I let her watch twenty minutes of Sesame Street. *I know she can't really learn from it yet, but I NEED the twenty minutes to nurse, get her dinner on the table, and—I admit— sometimes scroll through my messages.*

I am worried about the battles looming ahead. I am already dealing with tantrums when I turn the screen off (unless I'm strategic enough to pre-empt it with an enticing activity, but I am not a

magician). And I do hear the censorious voices: I'm ruining my child's
attention span, ability to play, imagination, college aspirations. But
sometimes it's, honestly, either screen time or scream time! What's a
reasonable middle ground?

Rest assured, you are NOT the only one. Most parents are using
screen time in their kids' early years as a "mother's helper" or unpaid
babysitter. When my son was about one and a half years old, in the
era of TV—lightyears before we talked about "screens"—we had no
TV at home (holding the then-common belief that TV is bad for
young kids). One day, we visited friends who did have a TV. My son
pointed at it and said "Babysitter!"

Most of the grandparents reading this book grew up watching
at least two hours of TV every day, some much more. Most of them
turned out fine, as did today's parents who grew up with about the
same amount of time daily, split between TV and video games.
That said, undoubtedly, the proliferation of screens, their addictive
interactivity, and the endless stream of information have made
the problem much more acute. Most adults who are honest with
themselves will admit to at least a hint of addiction—an urgency to
check the inflow of messages, tweets, information. Therefore, it's
perfectly reasonable to be more concerned about screen time now
than had been warranted in years back.

That is why I am putting this chapter about screen time in this
book's Babies and Toddlers section. It does, often, start that early.
Let's begin with four simple points:

1. Before age three (maybe even later), kids don't really learn
    from watching a screen. They need to play and learn with
    their bodies.

2. Screen time for toddlers and preschoolers is an asset for
    the parent/s, not the kid/s. In moderation, that's perfectly
    fine and reasonable. Who doesn't need fifteen minutes of
    downtime, with a child occupied so you can cook, clean,
    nurse, prepare a bottle, grab a bite, even... rest.

3. Screen time should play a very minor role in a young child's life. Most of the time, your child should be immersed in the physical play in "real reality." To paraphrase owl's advice to Ernie: "You gotta put down the iPhone if you want to play the saxophone."

4. Parents are modeling screen interactions all the time, and most of them are glued to their screens way too much.

So here are some suggestions for a sane, moderate approach:

1. For kids under age three: screen time of about fifteen minutes once or twice a day is fine: select appropriate programs. I won't cite any but the classic *Sesame Street* and *Mr. Rogers' Neighborhood (*also the now re-imagined as *Daniel Tiger's Neighborhood),* because they are popular and newer ones change too fast.

2. Pick the peak stress times for you and deploy screen time then.

3. Give your child clear markers when the program will end and close the screen promptly or, better yet, let him hit the "Off" button or close the laptop.

4. For ages four and five: Select half-hour age-appropriate programs (be careful about the scary ones: see the chapter on "Nightmares and Scary TV Programs" in the School-Age section). If possible, use screen time to accomplish other goals. For instance, you could say that cleanup time comes *before* screen time and needs to be done without repeated cajoling. Or you can make screen time the start of a slowing down/calming down routine before bedtime or after getting home from a very active day at preschool. Your child's screen time is your window to prepare dinner, clean up, and check your email.

5. At least some of the time, watch the programs with your child and talk about what happens (using "pause") or talk after it ends. It's talking things through that will really enhance your child's learning from what they are watching.

6. School Age: Screen time needs to be more fine-tuned now, divided between passive (watching programs) and interactive (surfing, texting, and social media, which you need to *supervise vigilantly* for age-appropriate content). You can offer your child a global amount of time for weekdays (sixty minutes *after* homework and chores are completed) and double or triple it for weekends (depending on her obligations), to divide however she wishes.

7. Every day (amount of time differing for weekdays and weekends), there should be a *screen-free time* for the *whole family* (yes, you too!). Ideally, this would be at least an hour, encompassing dinner and time following it (up to kids' bedtime would be optimal unless, as mentioned before, screen time is part of the end-of-the-day routine). I know that's hard! I recommend you discipline yourself to put your iPhone out of reach (in the bedroom, closet, even a box you lock so you need to go to some effort to retrieve the key to open it). Build up to an hour in ten-minute increments and monitor your progress. It's very challenging!

8. If you are in a profession or life situation where you need to be available to see urgent messages at all times, it's tough to create screen-free time. I suggest having your partner monitor your phone for you for the designated hour. They will let you know if there's a true emergency and won't be sucked into the non-vital messages the way you would be.

9. Screen time is likely to be an ever-present struggle in your daily life, so try to schedule one vacation a year where there will be no internet service.

Remember that being with yourself, in quiet contemplation or observing your surroundings, is a vital skill for building an inner life. If you believe an inner life— a life of the mind and the heart— is important, start as early as possible.

More information here: https://www.nytimes.com/2019/11/04/ well/family/screen-use-tied-to-childrens-brain-development.html

Nudity

The heat of summer is here, and my twenty-months-old has become a 24-7 stripper. I've tried to entice her to stay clothed with cute dresses and skirts in her favorite colors (not only pink! Purple, yellow, and orange as well), and she eagerly puts them on first thing in the morning. But once breakfast is over, it's off with the clothes! It's one thing when we are home, but she'll strip in the park, grocery store, parking lot, at friends' houses... you name it.

I certainly don't want to make her uncomfortable about her body, but it's gone too far. It's embarrassing! And I do worry about the day when she gets a lurid look and inappropriate comment from someone. Where's the right balance, and how do I broach this?

Ah... the pleasures of sunny, hot locales. Here in Berkeley, California, where the fog rolls in most afternoons, budding nudists are discouraged by temperature. But, seriously, this is an important issue because overreacting could lead to your daughter developing unhealthy attitudes about her body, while just "letting it all hang out" is awkward and may invite, as you say, unwanted and damaging reactions.

At under two years old, your daughter is too young for any kind of explanation about "mean people" out there or complex social etiquettes. Stick to a very simple rule: "*You can be naked at home, but not in other places. At home you can be naked when you are playing, but not when we are eating dinner or have guests* [you decide]." Limit the home restrictions to three or four basic situations and ignore the nudity the rest of the time.

How many restrictions you'll impose at home depends on how comfortable you and your partner are with nudity. In some families, nakedness is nothing special. Parents don't mind if their kids see them naked when they come out of the shower, in bed, even sunning on a private deck. In other families, parents want to be covered up (to varying degrees) at all times. Either scenario is perfectly normal and healthy, and you need not sweat it. Your child will gradually adopt the family culture regarding nudity. The less you "preach" and the more you just do what comes naturally, the smoother things will go.

Now, even in "Clothing-On 24/7" families, many toddlers and preschoolers go through a nudist phase. It's a vital part of their learning about their bodies and satisfying their natural curiosity about sex differences (for a more in-depth discussion, see the chapter "Masturbation and Playing Doctor"). But sometimes it can be pretty awkward, so here are a few simple tips (beyond the rules I mentioned above):

1. Encourage the naked times to happen in a backyard with privacy and/or in rooms of the house not exposed to outsiders (and draw the curtains).
2. Comment about it as little as possible (especially if it makes you get uptight).
3. Enforce the home rules about activities requiring clothing, making sure there's plenty of time in the day when nudity is okay.
4. Keep the house on the cool side of you want to discourage nudity. The lower temperature will gently minimize the frequency and duration of naked times.
5. When you go out, dress your daughter in overalls with snaps, putting them on backward so that the snaps are on her back. Keep the shoulder straps snug. Some Houdinis will get out of anything, but most kids will let it be. You can also keep her hands busy with carrying things, a fanny pack she can zip and unzip, etc.
6. As your child matures, you can graduate to somewhat more involved explanations as well as rewards for complying with your instructions.

7. Lots of kids between ages four and six are curious about boys' and girls' different genitals and will find an opportunity to take a look. If you catch them in the act, don't panic, don't faint, don't lecture. Very matter-of-factly say: "When we have guests, we stay dressed in our clothes. So, everybody put your clothes on now." You'd be wise to inform the other kid's parents, in a non-alarmed way.

Next play date, keep an eye out and, meanwhile, use pictures or anatomically correct dolls to educate your child. That said, repeated and frequent stripping when your child seems like she "has to do it" may be a signal of some trouble brewing, possibly due to exposure to age-inappropriate behavior or visual material. If you have the hunch this may be the case, don't just "let it go," but consult with a child therapist.

Traveling with Young Children

I am looking forward to bringing my three-months-old baby back to my parents' home to meet our big family. But I am worried about every detail, from flying to sleeping when we get there, plus the onslaught of unsolicited advice from everyone. What do you recommend?

Traveling with young children can be very challenging, so hopefully, this chapter will smooth the ride. The younger the infant, the smaller their orbit: all your baby needs is your (and your partner's) body and attention, readily available. If you fly, have the baby sucking vigorously (breast, bottle, pacifier, or your pinky) during takeoff and landing. It helps relieve the pressure in the inner ear. But, as almost everyone has experienced, it doesn't always work. Some babies just wail. Prepare your most charming smile and innocent shoulder shrug.

Jet lag can be a real challenge, too. Assume a minimum of one day per hour of time difference for adjustment. When my kids were little and we flew all the way to Israel, it was brutal. I had never imagined visiting the cows at 2:00 AM.

As a baby gets older, she depends on a larger array of objects to make her comfortable in her environment, so bring along a favorite musical mobile, sound machine, or some other portable item from her room. If you'll be schlepping a port-a-crib with you, you might get your baby adjusted to sleeping in it at home for a week before your trip. Hopefully, it'll make it easier on the other end.

When visiting with young children, I recommend arranging for them to sleep in the room with you. If you expect howling at bedtime and/or the middle of the night, give the grandparents (or other hosts) fair warning. The general rule I advocate about not immediately picking up your baby when he fusses holds at home, but it can be abrogated when traveling. Just go with the "path of least resistance" and assume you'll need "corrective training" for a week when you're back home.

The best response to unsolicited advice is a charming smile and "Thank you. I'll think about it," or "We might try that once we get home." Do think about it, and remind yourself of the good intentions behind the unwelcome tips.

Planning a trip *without* your child? I have a few tips for you as well. I do *(enthusiastically)* recommend overnights away from children every few months, as long as you have familiar sitters (grandparents, regular babysitter, a preschool teacher). That said, bear in mind this rough guideline: one night away for every year of age.

For kids over three and trips over two or three days:

1. Keep everything else in your child's routine as unchanged as possible.
2. Make a box with a compartment for each day you'll be gone (you can fasten together shoe boxes), putting a T-shirt, a photo of you, a small toy, and a short letter in each one. Your child should start each day with a new T-shirt and getting the "treasures" of the day. This will show him very concretely when you'll be back.
3. Buy postcards your child would like (e.g., animals, trains—

old-fashioned but still better than sending photos from your trip, even a video chat) before you depart and write on each one. Have your babysitter/parents put one (with a used stamp) in the mailbox each day. It's okay to pretend it came from you up to age five. Past that, you probably can't pull off this little deception.

4. Make a short video of you and your child snuggling, reading a favorite story, *before* you leave on your trip. Your child can watch it when she misses you the most.

5. Don't overdo the presents you bring back. Doing so would distract from the key task at hand—reconnecting emotionally.

6. Be prepared: when you come back, you may get the silent treatment or angry tantrums. These are to show you what it felt like to be left. Be patient, and keep hugging. It will pass.

Finally, one more rule while you are away: no more than 30 minutes twice daily for talking about your kid or kids. The rest of the time is for YOU. Wherever you go, have a good trip!

PART II: The Preschool Years

1. Sleep and Waking

Night Terrors

My three-year-old son has been waking up in the middle of the night, screaming at the top of his lungs. We rush to his room and find him sitting in his bed bolt up, eyes wide open, still screaming, but he doesn't respond much to our presence or comforting. He can scream for ten or fifteen minutes straight, and nothing we do calms him down. We've tried talking to him, holding him (he flails about if we try it), a drink of water, turning a light on, with no results. Then, suddenly, for no rhyme or reason, he stops, lies down, and is back asleep in a few minutes. In the morning, we check and find nothing wrong with him: he's his normal, cheerful self, no worse for the wear. We, however... are a different story. A couple of times, I have asked him if something hurt or scared him at night, but he seemed to have no memory of the screaming episode, and I don't want to "give him ideas" and exacerbate the situation. Help! We go to sleep with fear and trembling.

What you are describing is a classic manifestation of "night terrors," a different phenomenon from nightmares (more on those further down). It can be terrifying for parents, but seems not just unremembered but also harmless for the child. Let's begin with a description of its main features and then lay out your action plan.

Night terrors may be rather common. Experts' reports vary: some say they occur in less than ten percent of children, while others say about forty percent of children will have at least one episode. They occur in adults as well, more rarely, and are associated with other sleep disturbances such as sleepwalking. When they do come, it feels like all hell has broken loose.

Night terrors most commonly occur first around age three and usually pass of their own accord in a few months. But I have heard of both toddlers and school-age children having them for the first time. Sometimes they will come and go in clusters of four to five episodes over a couple of weeks, which then repeat every two to three months. The cause is unknown beyond their description as sudden waking in the deeper parts of the sleep cycle (most often during non-REM sleep), usually in the first third of the night. (Nightmares, like dreams in general, occur during REM sleep, usually toward the end of the night or the end of the typical four-hour sleep cycle.) The child doesn't fully awaken, which is why your son seems unaware of your presence and isn't comforted by your soothing. Even though a person may seem terrified during the night terror, there is usually no memory of the episode, even in older children and adults.

As I said, there is no clear medical evidence about what causes it. Some evidence suggests intense arousal during the day, such as stress and anxiety as well as positive excitement, intense activity (especially closer to bedtime), a period of sleep disruption or deprivation, fever, or perhaps a genetic disposition (ask around in the family). But really... we don't know, so don't over-investigate the cause.

So, what are parents to do?

1. First, try to take it in stride and realize that it's not anything

you are doing. Remember, it's much more disturbing (and disruptive) to you than to your child.

2. Plan on minimal intervention when your child wakes up. Basically, you just need to be in his room to make sure he doesn't hurt himself and wait it out.

3. You can try to hold his hand (though some kids will jerk their hand out): if that helps calm him, great! Or you can go the other direction and try to startle him out of it by turning on a light or music—fairly loudly. Try it. If it works, you've got a method; if not, abandon it after three tries.

4. If your son is having a lot of these episodes (say three or more per week) for a sustained period, track when they happen. If it's relatively predictable (e.g., three to three-and-a-half hours after he's fallen asleep), gently wake him up about fifteen minutes before you'd expect it: just enough for him to grumble, take a sip of water and turn to the other side. This may lighten his sleep and prevent an episode. This is a temporary measure: try it during phases of intense night terrors, but avoid making it into a regular pattern.

5. You can also experiment with reducing all the possible causes listed above. Some, such as reducing stress, fatigue, and overexcitement, would be beneficial in general, even if they don't prevent the night terrors.

6. In extreme cases—in terms of intensity, frequency, and duration—medical intervention (such as mild sleep-regulating medication) may be called for: consult your pediatrician and/or a sleep specialist.

Nightmares

And now, as promised, a few comments about nightmares. These, too, often start around this age. Perhaps not the dreams themselves (they may occur in infancy already) but the language skills needed to describe them. Typically, a child will wake up in the latter part of the night and cry out for you. He may be able to describe the content of the nightmare, but often will only be able to say it was scary. What to do?

1. Assure your child, "It was a bad/scary dream. It didn't really happen." Remember that, as in the case of monsters, there are things that are not real, but the fear of them certainly is.

2. At night, you don't want long discussions, so just tell your child, "I am here now, so you won't be scared. Go to sleep now." Stay in the room until he's drifted back to sleep. Sometimes, if your child's adrenaline has kicked in, that could be a while. Having a comfortable soft chair, couch, or camping mattress you can snooze on will ease things.

Sometimes, after a particularly scary nightmare of which your child has a vivid memory or several nights of nightmares in a row, a child develops anxiety about sleep and has a hard time falling asleep after a new nightmare or even at the beginning of the night. You can't guarantee a night without a bad dream, but the following ideas might help, by the power of suggestion:

1. In the middle of the night, tell your child, "You've already had the nightmare. You won't have the same one twice in one night."

2. At or before bedtime, talk about a possible nightmare (one he might have had already) and plan what he will dream to get himself out of it. For example, if his nightmare is that a robber is chasing him down the street, he could try to dream he has a rocket that propels him into the air and shoots lava at the robber so he can't chase him. Don't overdo it with the fantasies... the point is to reassure your child he has something ready in his "dream kit" to counter the nightmare.

3. For kids under four, at the height of magical thinking, you can take more concrete actions, like any one of the following:

    •   a poster on the door that says "No scary dreams allowed in this room"

- an anti-nightmare spray bottle
- a new toy of a fierce animal (lion, tiger, or Tyrannosaurus Rex) to sleep with, who'll protect against the scary things in the dreams

Morning Battles

Our four-year-old, generally sweet and cooperative girl takes FOREVER to get ready in the morning. She dawdles—she could be in the Olympics for that! Getting dressed is the hardest. She LOVES lingering in her PJs; she'd stay in them until noon every day. Is there a gene for that? Because I know she has no information about how I spent my weekends BK: before kids. PJs finally off, she spends twenty minutes picking an outfit and constantly gets distracted, "forgetting" how to do things she'd mastered a year ago. I must focus on getting my two-year-old ready as I prepare both kids for preschool solo. My husband has a long commute so, lucky guy, he leaves before "crunch time."

Things quickly deteriorate into my hurrying my daughter along and both of us getting frustrated. Recently she's started yelling, "Go away!" at me. I don't approve of this language, but I'm so frustrated I've yelled back: "I AM going away!" and left her to stew (and cry...). It all started in September when her little brother began attending her preschool, though she was very excited about it (and they both love the school). Getting two of them ready just threw a monkey wrench in our routine. Our mornings are chaos!

I have tried everything—more special time and cuddling with her on the one hand, being stricter and "giving consequences," on the other. I confess I've also tried bribes and threats... Nothing is working!

How can something be so frustrating and yet so common? You are in the same boat as the majority of parents who have to get their kids dressed, fed, bundled, and in the car or stroller before 8:00 AM.

I suspect it started in September not only because of the double duty but also because, proud of being a big sister as she is, your daughter was a bit jealous sharing "her school." I bet her brother is awfully cute too and steals some of the limelight.

The key here is changing the behavior patterns that now rule your morning with simple, clear directions and rewards for cooperation. Here's how:

1. Make the morning routine as simple as possible. Move what you can to the night before: preparing lunches (*with* your kids), putting jackets on hooks by the door, and so on.

2. Make a poster, with your kids' help, drawing or pasting pictures showing the morning routine with a box each for: dressing, breakfast, tooth and hair brushing, jacket on, lunch box in hand, buckling into the car seat or stroller (thirty minutes for a maximum of six steps). You can buy ready-made charts like this, but making it together with your child makes it ten times more powerful.

3. Explain the poster and say that from now on, you want them to follow the order each morning, nicely and cooperatively.

4. Help your daughter to move through the tasks by using a set of songs (the same every morning) to mark during which songs she must complete each task.

5. After she's completed all the steps and is ready for school, let your daughter use the time left (ten minutes is optimal) for a favorite activity (something not too hard to stop...) and help your son finish his tasks. He'll probably want to be on the same program. Great! It will help him learn to get ready more independently.

6. Create a sticker chart (or marbles/penny jar) explaining: "When you get ready for school like I ask, you'll get a sticker. For five stickers in a row, you get a small reward; for ten, a bigger one." Decide on the rewards yourself or let her choose, within your parameters. At first, rewards should come often, but then encourage working for bigger ones: it develops the capacity for delayed gratification—a key tool for building a civilization.

7. Have her pick her outfit the night before. The best time for this is when she is motivated to finish: before story-time or her favorite TV show (if it's part of your routine).

8. Tell her that PJs are for the weekend and let her stay in them as long as she likes, even if she goes back to bed in the PJs she woke up in. Join her in "PJ weekend" on special occasions.

9. Turn her "Go away!" into a question: "Do you want me to go away?" Say in a neutral tone (only if it's safe for you to leave): "Okay, I'll leave now. Call me when you're ready."

10. On day one of this program, start everything ten minutes earlier than usual.

11. Announce that when two weeks have gone smoothly, you'll have a party with special treats or a favorite family activity.

I hope it's "Party Time" soon!

II. Behavior, Family Relations, Bodies and Emotions

Temperament: Explosive, Reserved, and Painfully Shy

*M*y four-year-old son is generally a charming, loving boy, but sometimes he seems like a tinder box. If something sets him off, he can go from calm and collected to an exploding hand grenade in three seconds. Sometimes I can predict the explosion and head it off, but I worry about appeasing (dare I say, bribing) him too often. Other times, I am totally unprepared, and he, too, seems surprised, even shocked, by the intensity of his emotions.

I feel particularly unprepared to handle his outbursts because his brother, three years older, was the exact opposite at this age: very cautious, almost aloof, slow to warm up to people and situations, and always polite and cooperative. If anything, I needed to encourage him to be more assertive and "get out there" and almost hoped for an occasional tantrum, so I could assure him it was okay to lose it *once in a while (as, of course, I do). What's going on, and how should I respond?*

This chapter is crucial as a background *before* we delve into topics related to children's behavior and social interactions. It will serve you well to reflect on the basic foundation you are working with as a parent: your child's temperament. You are fortunate to have two boys with such different temperaments—they show you that it's not primarily about your parenting, but rather about who they are as people. Temperament is not only foundational and generally a given at birth, but it is also often inherited. Look around your family: whom does each of your boys remind you of? How have those people, presumably adults by now, negotiated life with their inborn temperaments? Can they be of help to you and your boys?

Start by realizing that one of the things that makes it hard for a parent to respond effectively to a child's temperament is a mismatch. If, say, a parent is an outgoing "life of the party" type and a child is socially cautious, let alone painfully shy, it's going to be hard to respond empathically and effectively. Similarly, if a parent who is always level-headed and cool as a cucumber has a child with an explosive temperament, there will be a "clash of cultures." The parents will likely find it very challenging to understand the child's reactions and behavior. So start mapping temperaments in your family, see who has what particular strengths and weaknesses, and make your plan based on this.

For a reserved or painfully shy child

1. If you were shy at some point (in early childhood or adolescence or after a move to a new community), use that experience to empathize with your child. Tell him about that period in your life, how you felt then and what being shy made you think about yourself. Correct the negative messages shyness often induces with an example from your or someone else's life, such as: "Because I was too shy to speak in class, the other kids thought I wasn't smart. But

then when I got A's on all the math quizzes, they saw how wrong they were."

2. Meanwhile, you or your naturally outgoing partner can act as a coach with some tricks of the trade on entering awkward social situations. These may include picking one child in the class to befriend (not the most popular one), starting with one-on-one playdates, rehearsing at home what to say during "show and tell," or role-playing asking to join a game.

3. Support your child by acknowledging how hard it is to be in new social situations. Plan limited exposure to such situations and carefully calibrate how much you push your child to manage them. Pick group activities with clear, even strict rules such as kids' martial arts. Those are easier on a shy child. Before the activity, review with your child what might happen and how he'd react. Afterward, go over everything that happened, noting especially the moments when he overcame his shyness. Let him know you noticed it and applaud him. But don't overdo the praise: don't tell him he's the bravest person on the planet because he kicked the ball when it rolled toward him.

4. Stay away, at least for a while, from activities that tend to be free-for-alls. These include games of chase or hide-and-seek in the park, chaotic, bounce-off-the-walls parties, some dance and music classes.

For an emotionally explosive child

1. Start by carefully observing what triggers your child. There are many likely culprits: frustrated wishes, fatigue, hunger, crowds, noise, too much tactile stimulation, too many demands in a row (e.g., "Put away your toy cars, wash your hands and sit at the table for dinner" all in one run-on sentence), impatient adults (who isn't impatient at the end of a long workday?) and demanding (annoying?) siblings.

2. Once you have a list of triggers, try heading them off in

advance. For example, if your child is more likely to explode when he's hungry, give him a snack *before* you ask him to do something or transition from one activity to the other.

3. Make a four-color chart with your child: green, yellow, orange, and red, assigning an emotional state to each. Green is "cool as a cucumber": draw a cucumber with a smiley face and ask your child for examples of when he's felt that way. Yellow is annoyed: give it a name, draw or cut a picture from a magazine (or print from the internet) of a slightly irritated face. Give examples, including when you are annoyed. Continue with orange for angry and red for furious/explosive.

4. Elicit and write down your child's ideas for how to move the dial down from red to orange (e.g., pummel a punchbag, go to his room and scream his head off), orange to yellow, and yellow to green.

5. Now start the action plan: naming how he and you are feeling by colors at many points during the day. Emphasize the moments when he's green and, even more importantly, when he succeeds in down-shifting from one color to the one a level below it. Provide suggestions on how to do this, such as taking five deep breaths, counting to twenty, reciting a funny poem, breaking into a silly dance, or making crazy faces.

6. Use the chart to track and encourage emotional control by putting stars or stickers on the chart each time you note your child is successfully shifting down emotionally.

7. Have an agreed-upon strategy for the explosive moments, giving your child permission to blow off steam in acceptable ways that don't cause bodily harm or destroy your furniture. Examples include pouncing on and punching a bop bag, tearing up and crumpling newspapers and throwing them around the room (to be collected later in a basketball game later, when the storm has passed), and throwing/piling pillows onto the couch.

8. Make a reentry plan, too: once your child has calmed down, he needs a face-saving way of coming back to civilized society and into your arms. This will likely include a hug, an apology (from him and you), and quiet time together. The reentry would be helped along by reading a book that captures some of your child's experience, such as *Spinky Sulks* by William Steig or *Alexander and the Terrible, Horrible, No Good, Very Bad Day* by Judith Viorst.

9. Finally, if you, too, have your red-hot moments, model for your child by:

    •   Naming it: "I am so angry I need to stop myself and calm down."

    •   Taking steps to deescalate: "I am going to take a deep breath and listen to music with earphones for a few minutes."

    •   Re-entering when you've collected yourself: "I am calm now. Let's figure out together what to do here."

Take some deep breaths and go for it.

Dawdling, Timers, and "Five More Minutes"

My three-year-old son is a champion dawdler. I can't get him to go along promptly with any of my plans. Everything is a struggle. On good days it's repeated negotiations for "five more minutes;" on bad days, I alternate between shouting and bribing.

It's hard enough getting him to cooperate so we can leave on time in the morning for daycare (while I don't have to punch a clock, punctuality is highly valued at my job and coming late is always noted). Often, he'll resort to saying he hates his daycare. But I know that's just a tactic to delay our departure because when I pick him up at the end of the day, it's as big a struggle to get him to leave. The problem repeats at home for mealtime, bath time, and, of course, bedtime. On weekends, it's just as bad: getting dressed to leave for an outing, leaving to go to the park, or time to get off the swing.

I generally give him a five-minute warning and will often agree to "just five more minutes," but I suspect he has no concept of how long that actually is. I am torn between taking a much harder line and showing him that when I say it's time to stop/go/leave, it is time, right then and there, versus a reward-based approach—using a timer and giving him rewards for cooperating. Which would you recommend, and how do I get him to understand how much "five more minutes" means?

Let's start with the basic understanding that our hurried, time-ruled lifestyles are totally at odds with the natural inclination of young children. Left to his own devices, your son might one day want to spend three hours playing in his bed before he gets up, but the next morning he could spring out of bed, put his clothes on (to the best of his ability), and pester you to go out before you've even had a chance to go to the bathroom, let along get breakfast ready.

There are two important elements to this mismatch of kids' time and our adult clock:

1. What we adults see as dawdling is often that semi-dreamy state of free play, when a child is in their own imaginary world and our action-packed, time-sensitive agenda is an unwelcome interference. It's a crucial element of child development (see the chapter on "Free Play").

2. Adults have a clear concept of the passage of time, based on years of experience and watches on our wrists (or phones), while for a child under age five, "five minutes" is a vague concept that generally simply means "hurry up."

Ideally, we would provide ample opportunities for young children to *pace themselves* and decide on their own when one activity is completed and it's time to move on to another. But since our lives tend to have inadequate leisure, that's more aspirational than realistic. So try to do the following:

1. Carve out more leisure time during the weekend: at least half a day of unhurried play with no timetable.

2. During the workweek, if your schedule is extremely pressured in the morning, bite the bullet and get up twenty to thirty minutes earlier than you do now, to build in at least a little time for dawdling.

3. Streamline your morning routine to minimize the number of tasks you and your child have. For example, pack lunch the night before and have the lunchbox ready in the fridge. Have your child sleep in the clothes he'll wear to daycare the next day. If you take a stroller, have it packed and ready to go with jacket/fleece on the handlebar.

4. Follow the morning routine tasks in the same order each morning, so your child internalizes the sequence.

5. If the morning is a big struggle, work into the routine—at the very end, right before leaving—something your child really enjoys that has a definite ending, such as reading one storybook selected the night before or watering the plants (fill the watering can the night before). If *your* morning routine is complex (with two or more kids or special tasks you have to accomplish), and especially if a partner is not on hand to help, the last activity can be watching a fifteen-minute TV program, while you get yourself or other kids ready.

6. *Use music instead of a timer.* A ticking timer means very little to your child; they have no concrete concept of what three or five minutes mean. Instead, put on two or three short songs they like. It's better to use the same songs every time or have a limited "playlist:" two cheerful songs for morning time, two songs for cleanup, two for getting ready for the bath, and two quiet songs for winding down and getting ready for your going-to-sleep routine. When you are at the playground, play the songs on your phone or, better yet, sing them!

7. Finally, about rewards. These can be very helpful at the beginning of the training process when you're trying to inculcate more timely transitions. Start with small rewards,

such as a sticker or a tiny toy animal that you give your child immediately upon completing the task/transition promptly. Next, move on to a chart with squares for each small step needed (e.g., clean up toys during two songs, get undressed and into the bath during the next two songs) with a checkmark or star for each one. At the end of the day, count the stars and tell your child they've done a good job. Show them how they are improving from day to day and tell them that when the chart has X number of stars on it, they'll get a bigger reward. Pick a modest one to start with (e.g., a toy car, small stuffed animal). As your child gets the hang of it and matures, replace the immediate rewards with a point system, working toward something bigger that your child has their heart set on.

8. Remember that this is a learning curve, so give your child (and yourself) some extra time. Thus, for example, start by focusing on the morning routine and get up at least fifteen minutes earlier than usual. Do the same at the end of the day at daycare if that's a tough transition. Come ten minutes early (if you can) and allow your child to show you two things he played with/worked on that day before you depart.

As you implement this plan, ask yourself how pressured you are yourself by the ticking of the clock and look for ways to create more unhurried spaces in your own life. Both you and your child will benefit.

Limit Setting

We have two kinds of" No!" battles in our house: either I say "no" and my kid just keeps doing whatever I told her not to do, or I tell her to do something (I try to model asking politely) and she says" no." Between those two versions of" no," I don't know what to do to get more cooperation and peace. As you can imagine, these exchanges turn into temper tantrums, sometimes as often as ten times a day.

Of course! I can't count the number of parents who've told me: "I say 'no' and have a temper tantrum on my hands." This is especially likely when your "no" is followed up by swiftly taking away the knife/porcelain vase/TV remote control/iPhone away from eager, exploring hands. Almost as many ask how they can get their child to "do what they're told" as ask how to respond to their child's defiant "No!"

Setting limits is a continuous task (sometimes better described as" battle") to protect your children from danger and your possessions from destruction, while also teaching what we think of as the "building blocks" of civilization. Young children need limits:

1. To be and feel safe in the world around them
2. To help manage uncontrollable emotions that easily overwhelm them
3. To know they can always rely on their parents (and other caretaking adults) for their security
4. To learn how to deal with frustration and anger using words, not aggression.

Ensuring physical safety is obvious, though not always easy. We put up safety gates, lock away chemicals and medicines, hold our child's hand walking down the street. It comes naturally; you know you've got to do it. Harder are the daily struggles over rules and parents' instructions, managing explosive emotions at home (and preschool or daycare) in an effective and nurturing manner.

Young children's emotions are extremely intense. Their joy is unbounded; their rage is fearsome! They, themselves, can get frightened by the intensity and explosiveness of their feelings. They need adults to confirm and reconfirm the rules, model and set limits on how to express intense emotions, and stop them from hurting others or themselves (more about aggression in another section). They derive their sense of security from the adults around them, including—even especially—when the adults say "no."

Limit setting must be consistent and firm. It is an integral part of the separation-individuation process, whereby a child becomes her own independent person, beginning with the birth of "no." All the adults in the family and childcare/preschool staff, hopefully, agree on the same rules and stick to them faithfully. Rules get modified gradually as a child matures, but changing the rules in the moment should be reserved for extraordinary circumstances only.

As pedantic as it may seem, *writing down your rules* can help both you and your child. Even a toddler, years away from reading, will respond to you reading the rules out loud (stick to only two or three). Make a small poster, illustrated with stick figures or pictures from magazines or printed from the internet.

Toddlers have not yet developed their language skills well, but their determination to "do it by myself" is at an early peak. So you can avoid at least some meltdowns by offering a choice between two options, where both are equally acceptable to you. For example, if you tell your child "Put this shirt on," you're in for a struggle, but if you offer her a choice between the red one or the blue one, she will be happy to exercise her power and independence. Once you have a tantrum on your hands, stay calm, make sure your child is safe, and stick to your rules. The next chapter will give you more detailed suggestions.

Temper Tantrums

Tantrums can start in infancy but are more typical for toddlers and preschoolers; they are a natural response to frustration. These key tips will help you manage them:

1. Help your child verbalize that anger in the moment, e.g., "I know you're *so* angry because Mommy took away the scissors. You cannot have them, though. It is not safe." Stay with your child and help them calm down by talking, holding them, handing them their stuffed animal, or letting them snuggle in an armchair or bean bag in the corner of the room.

2. Don't back off from your action/rule and enforce it with physical action (removing an object from your child's hand

or the child from the trouble spot). Repeat and explain the rules *after* you child has calmed down.

3. Reassure your child: "Right now, you're still too mad, but when you feel better, we can ___." Suggest something your child really likes: reading a story, building a castle with blocks, playing dress-up, but *not* something out of the ordinary (ice cream at 10:00 AM, a trip to Disneyland). You don't want your child to get the idea that a tantrum is a way to get something special.

4. Stay close by. I am not in favor of "time out" in a separate room, at least not until age four or so, when kids have more tools to manage their emotions (the age will vary from child to child). "Time out" should mean being removed from the source of trouble (your laptop, window sill, hot stove), and only the minimal attention needed to let your child know you're present and ready to help them calm down. Beware of giving so much attention as to make it a "dramatic production."

5. Some kids do best if you hold them in an enveloping hug, while others escalate if you try to do that. The latter kids may need a rug to roll on and kick, a big armchair to flail around on, or a pillow to punch.

6. After the storm passes, teach your child the words they need, such as "angry, mad, sad, frustrated." Make a chart with drawings or pictures of those facial expressions, play games where you take turns *pretending* to be angry or sad, and ask, "What can we do so I don't feel so mad/sad?" Engage your child in suggesting possibilities: a big hug or a kiss, holding a beloved stuffed animal, punching a bob-bag, tearing up and crumpling newspapers, stomping your feet.

7. Distraction and humor (making silly faces, starting a silly song), can help shorten the tantrum's duration and intensity. But when kids approach age four, they may well be insulted by this, as you seem to be making fun of their raging storm. Back off.

Sometimes a child's tantrum is so intense it sets you off. Have you ever felt like throwing a tantrum yourself? Or yelling at your child, or... even hitting? Feeling like that once in a while is a common part of parenting. If you do lose your cool with your child, be sure to address it. Tell them: "I am so sorry I yelled at you. I was too angry when I did. It makes me feel sad now." And it's okay to say "I need a little time out to calm down," and model by taking demonstrative deep breaths, counting out loud to ten, or closing your eyes (if it's safe to leave your child unwatched for a few seconds) and hugging a pillow to your chest.

But, if you "lose it" often, you need more help. Talk to a therapist, a child development specialist, your pediatrician, or a support group. And know that you are not alone.

Toilet Training

My two-and-a-half-year-old son loves to read the potty-training books we have (I admit... it's a small library), but when I suggest he actually use the potty, he declines. Sometimes he says he's too busy now and others he says, "When I am older."

I don't want to push him and make it into a battle, but I wonder when and how to encourage him. Some of his friends are already toilet trained and others not. I hear so much contradictory advice and strategies. I am confused. What's a sensible middle-of-the-road approach?

There are so many books and advice sites about toilet training that this is going to be a short chapter; no need to add to the sea of literature. Start by reading the chapter "Potty Training: Stickers vs. M&M's" in Emily Oster's book, *Cribsheet.* It won't tell you how to proceed but *will* calm you down. She demonstrates that data-driven research shows no differences in eventual outcomes (namely educational success, emotional well-being, and success in adulthood tasks) between achieving toilet training by a child-led approach or by a parent-initiative with rewards. So think about the following issues in deciding what's best for your child and your family:

1. Your child's temperament: is he easygoing and cooperative or determined, even tending toward the obstinate?

2. What developmental stage is he in now? Is he in a cooperative mode or a defiant one?

3. How developed are his verbal and reasoning skills? Can he fully understand cause and effect, motivational rewards?

4. How harried or leisurely is the daily routine of the adults in the family? Can you afford the close attention needed for supporting/encouraging parent-led toilet training now and dealing with accidents? Would it, honestly, be much easier to just keep him in diapers for longer, until he has more initiative and self-control and toilet training can be completed much faster?

5. Is he in a daycare or preschool where he can learn the ropes by watching his peers and using the toilet at set times?

6. Is he in or about to enter a preschool class where he must be toilet-trained to start (so there is some time pressure on the matter)?

7. Are you expecting a baby in the next few months?

8. Is some other major life transition on the horizon (moving, starting a new daycare arrangement, dramatic changes in your or your partner's work schedule)?

Put all these ingredients in a big pot, add your and your partner's intuitive inclination, stir briskly, and let it settle. Pick what you think will work best for your family and your present circumstances. Now do some reading on the approach you've picked (but not too much—it might confuse you again or stress you out) and follow its step-by-step plan. Be sure to:

1. Pick a plan you are comfortable with.

2. Implement it with reasonable dedication (at a low-stress time for your family).

3. Prepare for it to take some time (usually several weeks at least,

less with an older child) and be ready for and nonchalant about accidents and missed opportunities.

4. If you are out and about a lot with your child, have a rule that in the beginning, he wears diapers on outings. Using the toilet at someone else's house or a public place is a big step: reserve it for later.

5. Keep a clear distinction—in your mind and in explaining it to your son—between daytime toilet training and nighttime. For many kids, there is a gap of many months (sometimes well over a year) between the two stages. Don't start suggesting nighttime without diapers until your child consistently wakes up dry in the morning and initiates (or at least happily complies with you about) going to the toilet to pee.

6. If things don't go well, back off. What you want to watch out for and be sure to avoid is toilet training becoming a power struggle between you and your child.

At the risk of being repetitious: relax! Almost all children are toilet-trained, one way or another, before kindergarten, and that's a reasonable goal.

Masturbation and "Playing Doctor"

Our almost-four-year-old son has a close friend: our neighbor's daughter. They've known each other since they were toddlers. She's about his age, and they play together very well, sometimes for hours. Two weeks ago, I noticed they had been playing in his room for an unusually long time and surprisingly quietly. I went in and found them "playing doctor" with their clothes off. I tried to stay level-headed and said, "Time for a snack. Put your clothes on," and exited the room. They came out quickly, and had, I thought... but maybe I'm projecting... guilty little smiles on their faces.

I wasn't sure what to say, so I didn't address it. I did, however, let the girl's mom know about it. She didn't seem that concerned, but we have not received an invitation for a playdate at their house. The kids do usually play together at least once a week.

I should add that for a while now, I have noticed my son touching himself more often, but also a bit less openly. He tends to do it while reading books, piling pillows around himself, or while "talking" with his stuffed animals on his bed. I don't intervene. What should I do and what should I say—to my child, maybe the friend when she comes over, and to her mother?

Let's begin with a simple distinction between two versions of "playing doctor." The first is a form of pretend play to master feelings (mostly anxiety: see the chapter on "Going to the Doctor") about visits to the doctor and generally play-acting adult jobs such as teacher, firefighter, or police officer. That's not your concern here.

Your question is about the very common play driven by curiosity about bodies and sex differences. Kids get deeply interested in how their bodies work, starting around their third birthday. The exploration includes naming body parts (that, of course, begins much earlier), enjoying nudity (see a separate chapter on that), measuring feats of strength and speed, and, of course, checking how their own genitals work and how others' look.

The curiosity about genitals is a bit less intense in a family where a young child has occasion to see his parents naked and it's no big deal. Reading books about bodies and encouraging questions helps, too. But ultimately, most kids want to see and touch their own genitals and also their friends'. Masturbation, which can start as early as a child has enough control of their hands and body to touch themselves, is natural and healthy and is part of this journey of exploration (more on that further down).

So first of all, calm down: it's normal! Now take stock: Does your son feel comfortable with his body? Do you welcome his questions? Does he have books with realistic drawings about all his body parts? If not, there's your starting point.

As long as the doctor games are not:

1. The only thing he wants to play with his friend
2. Done in great secrecy
3. Involve more than "show and tell" of each other's genitals

then there is no cause for alarm. That said, you ought to talk to the girl's mother and find out her level of comfort with the situation and make a plan that works for both families.

Monitor a bit more closely what goes on during their playdates. If you and the other parents are not comfortable with the situation, set down some rules, such as:

1. When we play at each other's houses, we keep all our clothes on, all the time.
2. When we play together in either of our rooms, we keep the door open.
3. We talk about body parts we have questions about with our parents.
4. We never play in a way that makes one of us feel "icky" (uncomfortable).
5. We always say "stop" if we don't like how our friend wants to play and get an adult to help.

If your son seems stressed about this, he may be picking up negative messages from you, even if you try to look accepting. Be honest with yourself: is this advice making you feel uncomfortable? Would you rather restrict your child further? Think it through: assess what *your* baggage is and what is age-appropriate for your child. If you are too conflicted, do some more reading, consult with your child's pediatrician, and, perhaps, work with your own therapist to address issues this may be bringing up for you.

Now let's return to masturbation. It, too, is normal, is healthy, and... can make you very uncomfortable. Around age four is the time to gently redirect your son when he masturbates in front of people. You can say something like "Touching our bodies [or 'private parts,' or other terms you use at home] can feel nice, but it's something we do by ourselves." Explain, if it hasn't come up yet, what privacy is and give *another example* of something we do in private so that it's not *only* masturbation and he doesn't associate masturbation with toileting. This can be challenging. Consider: do you prefer to dress, shower, or put on makeup quietly and in private? Does your son have any other activities he likes to do by himself? It could be snuggling with his stuffed animals in his bed or talking to an imaginary friend.

There are, however, times when playing doctor or masturbation should be of concern. If you're wondering about either behavior, observe your child more carefully, and possibly seek professional advice. These are the key things to look for:

1. Your child masturbates a lot, seems to feel a compulsion to do it, or does it to the point of irritating the genitals.
2. Your child attempts to insert objects into the anus or genitals.
3. Your child can't take it to his room and continues to masturbate in the presence of others.
4. Your child gets visibly upset when you nudge him to do it in private.
5. Your child repeatedly touches other people (his peers or adults), be it on the genital area or the breasts.
6. Your child simulates sexual intercourse positions in either solitary play or with friends.

7. Your child coerces his peers (or younger kids) to play doctor or touch each other's bodies.

8. None of the above, but you just feel too uncomfortable about your child's sexual behavior.

These behaviors can be alarming and hard to discuss, even with your partner, let alone friends or your child's pediatrician or teachers. Few of us were raised with the support and freedom to acknowledge and discuss sexuality openly, so get some help!

Mommy-itis: When Your Child Wants Only Mommy (or Daddy)

My daughter has recently crossed my husband off her list: I am the only one who can comfort her or help her. I'm on duty 24/7: bedtime, dressing, buckling her car seat, spreading jam on her toast. I am torn between responding to her needy phase (not sure why...) and keeping my sanity. My husband is trying to stay above it, but it's hard on him.

First, relax. Periodical "Mommy-itis" or "Daddy-itis" is common. It often makes several appearances in early childhood (with a possible reprise in adolescence). Sometimes, in infancy, it seems like only one parent can soothe a baby when he is fussy or get him to sleep. In the toddler-preschool years, expect at least one such period, often coupled with other struggles about "who's boss." If you dig Freud, you will even welcome an oedipal period: a girl being "Daddy's girl" or a boy glued to Mom's side.

Let's take infancy first. It's natural for a nursing baby to form a stronger attachment to the mother in the early months of life. My daughter told me when she was about five, "I am closer to you because you milked me." Very often, without plan or notice, Mother becomes the "soother of choice." This is perfectly fine as long as you keep an eye on it. Make sure it does not become so exclusive that Dad (or second Mom) cannot put the baby down to sleep or soothe them when they are fussy. Your partner needs plenty of opportunities to bond with the baby and develop their own repertoire of soothing techniques.

Bigger struggles come once your child has the vocabulary to insist on only one or the other verbally. Here you need to think of the "only Mommy" demand on a continuum. Visualize the Golden Gate Bridge with the San Francisco side representing going along 100 percent with your child's demands and the Marin side as total stonewalling, in which the parents are "the deciders," never acceding to a child's preference. You want to be right around mid-span, where the gusts of wind from the ocean are strongest. Pardon the metaphor—the idea is that mid-span is the "happy medium," but the ups and downs are more intense. So, what do you actually do?

1. Accept that for a while, for whatever reason, your child needs you more intensely than she needs her dad. Do consider why that may be: Did you go out of town? Are you more stressed? Is your partner working harder so that your child picks up that he is less emotionally engaged?

2. For a while, do make yourself more available, but make sure to get breaks. Have your partner develop some simple new activities that are his "specialty," be it working in the garden, building bridges with Lego, collecting rocks, or breakfast on Sundays.

3. Evaluate how much of this is about control. Is your child in the midst of struggling to control every little detail (to compensate for a growing sense that she really controls very little)? Is she flipping out that you buttered the wrong side of the toast, so you *must* make a new one? Is everything, be it clothes, brushing teeth, going to bed, or whatever else, a battle? Probably...

4. Make a list of things that are "Choice" and those that are not. "Choice" allows your child to pick the parent they want, e.g., helping with pajamas, hair brushing, reading a specific book, etc. "No Choice" are daily activities that are vital for you to share with your partner, such as putting your child to bed, getting ready for preschool, driving places.

5. Explain to your child about "Choice" and "No Choice" and give her many opportunities to have "Choice" activities. You can amplify the impact with some silliness, such as: "If you could go to the moon, would you want to go with Mommy or Daddy?" or "If you stood on your head all day, would you want Mommy or Daddy to help you?" Encourage your child to invent other ideas like this. As these become sillier and sillier, you are defusing the intensity behind the struggle.

And—don't worry too much. If your child sees that she is not "yanking your chain" with the Mommy-itis, she will soon move on.

Becoming a Big Sister/Brother

We are expecting our second child in two months. Our two-year-old seems a bit baffled by the excitement, especially people telling her about becoming a big sister. To me, it looks like she's a bit intimidated by the idea of being "big," but maybe I'm reading too much into it. The hospital where we'll deliver has a program for siblings, and we plan to take our daughter there about a month before the due date. But, on the whole, I vacillate between thinking I am preparing her too much and worrying I am not doing enough. What do you suggest?

I suspect you are right on both counts, even though that's self-contradictory. On the one hand, telling a two-year-old about things that are going to happen more than a week or two out is more confusing than helpful. She's probably already heard from a lot of people about her baby brother or sister coming soon, and, yet, no baby has shown up! She's probably puzzled and possibly a bit worried about whether something has gone wrong. Kids younger than three only need three to four weeks of prep time, unless the pregnancy has significantly curtailed your range of activities with her. If that's the case, you have to explain it by focusing on tangible things like the size of your abdomen, not the misty future of a baby coming. From age three on, add more time, but be sure to use recognizable signposts, such as "after Christmas" or "Four weeks after your birthday."

There is a whole library of books for older siblings welcoming the new baby, and many of them are excellent, so I need not cover that. The most valuable ones address the child's mix of excitement about the new baby and the frustrations of parents' divided attention, the baby crying, and the disappointment that the baby is really not a playmate for what seems like forever. Pick two or three books you like and read those over and over. Repetition of a familiar text and pictures is more reassuring than reading a whole bookshelf. At least some of the time, when you read one of those books, stop at several pages and ask your child what she thinks: What will happen in the book? What will happen when *our* new baby comes?

Remember that your child's foremost question, whether she can articulate it or not, is not what will the baby be like, but "What will it be like for *me?*" So, you need to reassure her that her routines, her beloved toys, and her favorite activities and friends will remain the same, albeit with some interruptions when you need to take care of the baby. Plan and practice in advance a code word that she can say when she feels you're too busy with the baby and ignoring her. A big, funny word is best. I used "hippopotamus" with my son (he was just over three when his sister was born), and it worked beautifully, in part because he loved articulating every syllable and usually cracked up saying it.

Beyond the obvious plans you need to make to care for your daughter when you deliver, I suggest the following steps for before and after:

1. Just like you'll have a bag pre-packed with things you need to take to the delivery, get one ready for her (pack it together). Put in a few favorite books, a couple of small stuffed animals, and other soothing things she uses (including a pacifier if she's still got one), and a photo of you and her together.

2. Buy a stuffed animal or doll for her in advance of the baby's arrival and bring it with you from the hospital. Tell her it's "a present from the baby to you."

3. Get her a doll and play bottles, possibly also a doll stroller as well, and encourage her to play "mommy and baby" starting a few weeks before the baby's arrival.

4. Set up a "service station" in the living room within her easy reach, with diapers, an ointment jar/tube (screwed tight so she can bring it to you but not open it without your supervision), wipes, drool bibs and receiving blankets. This will be her "headquarters" for helping you when you're taking care of the baby. Remember to give simple directions, asking for one item at a time.

5. Thank her for helping, stating the specifics of what she does: "Thanks for bringing me a diaper," and don't overdo the "you are such a big girl," or "you are the best helper." That's too tall an order for her.

6. Prepare in advance a stash of small toys and books for when well-meaning visitors come and bring a gift for the baby, but not for her. Of course, the baby doesn't care about gifts, but your daughter does! When guests arrive, ask them discreetly if they have something for your daughter. If they are embarrassed that they hadn't thought of it, say, "hardly anyone does..." and hand them something from your stash.

7. Finally, try to arrange your schedule and support so that you can have fifteen minutes every day with just your daughter, when none of your attention is needed for the baby. It helps to name it "special time" and refer to it when your daughter gets impatient: "I know it's hard because I'm busy with the baby right now, but right after dinner, you and I will have our special time. What do you think you'll want to do together?"

Between these suggestions, getting as much hands-on help from family, friends, neighbors, and babysitters as possible, and being lucky enough to have a smooth delivery and healthy baby, you'll all survive!

Sibling Relations: Preschoolers and
Their Younger Siblings

We have two kids under age four, and sometimes it seems each one of them needs two parents. When their needs conflict, it's a bit of a circus. I can manage as long as they don't go at each other, but, of course, they do. Sometimes the four-year-old taunts his little sister, both verbally and physically. Anything she does, he'll show off he can do better, higher, faster. Often when she's playing with a toy he'd lost interest in ages ago, he'll snatch it from her and declare it's his (it was... two years ago). She is two, so her repertoire is either hitting him or crying. At other times, it's she who bulldozes her way through his intricate Lego construction, and he's a puddle of tears. Or she'll imitate him, and it drives him nuts, but he's helpless to stop it.

We had such lovely visions of them playing together, of the older boy teaching his sister how to build with blocks and the little one so proud of her big brother... Will we ever see that? What can we do to foster a loving sibling relationship instead of this constant rivalry?

This sounds very trying, but I can assure you it is nothing out of the ordinary. Managing siblings and fostering a peaceful, let alone loving, relationship at these young ages is an accumulation of short spurts of cooperation and love, not a straight, long stretch. But enough moments of siblings playing together happily in the park or (this one is the best!) comforting each other in moments of tears, build the foundation for life-long closeness and mutual support.

Thus, the first tip I have is: when moments of sibling harmony occur (even quick and simple ones), note them, remember them, document them with photos, and make them into stories. "Remember when Sally lost her doll, and Harry found it for her way, way under the bed?" You can even make a book of "Our Family's Stories" in which you record these moments. As your kids grow older, the stories will become more complex and daring, compassionate, and, hopefully, at least some of the time, amusing.

The second point to remember is that this is a particularly tough time. Your daughter is no longer a cute baby that stays put and adores her brother and his every move. She's a rival now: competing for toys, attention, your arms, everything. Neither of them has much self-control, so it's going to be very hands-on for another year or so. Once your son is five years old, he will likely be able to tolerate, manage, and outsmart his little sister's incursions, grabbing, and competition for attention with more patience and skill.

Now, take a few days to observe when the flare-ups are most likely to occur. The typical times and triggers are:

1. Late in the day or when you're rushing to get out.
2. When you are attending to something important other than your kids (phones are the most common culprit).
3. One or both kids being tired, hungry, or overstimulated (or getting sick).
4. There is no set routine for the period in the day when the flare-ups are most likely.
5. Something exciting being about to happen, but either they have to wait or getting ready takes a lot of steps.
6. A new game or toy.

Once you've mapped the frequency, timing, and triggers, you get to work on heading off at least some of them; you can't avoid them all.

Additional key factors in the equation are your available attention and your relationship with your partner. This is rather obvious but still worth mentioning. If you are very preoccupied with something important or distressing, your kids will feel it and react, increasing intensity in their rivalry. If you and your partner are feeling tense or angry with each other, your kids will feel that, too. Often, they will try (unconsciously) to defuse the tension and bring you and your partner closer together by enacting the hostility between them. This is likely to occur between older siblings as well (into the teen years and even adulthood).

Now for some quick, everyday tips:

1. Set up a spot in your house or apartment where the four-year-old can play and build, or at least put his creations out of reach of the toddler.

2. Make a visual representation of "patience" for your son. For example, his quotient of patience could be his height and his sister's hers, or his could be a basketball and hers a baseball. Use it to explain to him that when they both need you, most of the time, you'll take care of the toddler's needs first. Then explain that patience goes along with attention span. While you may do something with his sister for a few minutes and then she gets bored, he, four years old that he is, can play something "for hours" (a little exaggeration will help make him feel proud and therefore, at least sometimes, more patient). Map out with him how you'll divide your time and give him something to do while he waits.

3. Recruit your son to teach his sister simple games where he can be the guide and mentor. Let him know when he's done a good job teaching her something. Maybe he can "read" her a short bedtime story, too (from a book he has memorized)? He would love that role, and she would love her "story-time with big brother."

4. If your four-year-old goes to sleep after his sister, following her bedtime is a very special time for him. Devote at least twenty minutes (a bit more is better) to being with him (rather than attending to all the many things on your to-do list). However, sometimes it's the older child who goes to sleep earlier. If that's the case, find a different time, perhaps first thing in the morning, when he can have you to himself.

5. Arrange your schedule, at least on the weekend, so that each child has some one-on-one time with at least one parent.

6. Encourage but don't demand hugs and kisses and sweet words.

7. Read books about having a baby sister and sibling

relationships (there are many) and make your own book about it for your family.

The rest is just hard work, day in and day out, and a *lot* of patience. Compared to your kids' heights, yours will have to be about as tall as the Empire State building.

Gender Identity, Roles and Rules

"I want to be a boygle," my four-year-old son said to me.

"You want a bagel?" I asked.

"No, to be a boygle."

I racked my brain for the Yiddish words my mom has been teaching him, but nothing rang a bell. He has a bit of a lisp, so sometimes he's hard to understand. He gets very frustrated and hurt when we don't understand him, so I trod lightly.

"So, it's not something you want to eat... it's something you want to be..."

"Yes," he said empathically, "a boygle."

"Is that a character in a book or a game?" I was still floundering.

"No, Mommy!" He was getting upset.

"So," I said in my loving, empathic voice, "What is a boygle?"

"A boygle is a boy-girl. A boy who wants to be a girl."

"Oh, I get it. Interesting..." I said, trying to buy myself some time.

"You know," he said, "like Sara in my class, she is a gal-boy. But I want to be the opposite."

Now it registered. A parade of moments when Tommy wanted to wear his older sister's dress, walk in my high heels, and try my lipstick flashed through my mind. Not sure what to say, I used the fallback: "Tell me more about it."

After his list of the things he wanted to do as a "boygle," I retreated to another safe bet: "That's very important. Let me think about it, and we'll talk about it together with Daddy."

He seemed fine with my evasion and delay and went off to play

with his construction set, telling me, "I am building a princess' castle." I
rushed to write to you and then to the internet, where there is so much
information I feel confused. How should I proceed?

Let's begin by acknowledging that this is a new and challenging
territory for many parents. Thankfully, we are now much more
aware and attuned to gender identity as a spectrum, not a binary
proposition, but most of us don't have our childhood memories to
rely on for guidance. Speaking of that, let me share mine.

I grew up on a kibbutz in Israel in the days of collective education.
Children spent most of their time with their age group, including
sleeping at night in a children's house. We had only the afternoon
and early evening hours with our parents. Thus, peer pressure and
peer support were extremely important.

In third grade, I announced to my classmates that henceforth,
my name would be Danny, and I would be a boy. My classmates
were not shocked—there had been signs all along, especially my key
position on the soccer team, which, by third grade, was boys only.
They acquiesced (I had a fairly dominant personality at the time)
and made the switch. Only adults—our teacher, daytime caretaker,
and my parents—were allowed to call me by my old name, Racheli.

I am sure those adults were concerned... but no one ever said
anything to me. Years later, my mother, who had then been on her
way to becoming a child therapist, told me she instructed everyone
to ignore it, assuming it would pass. It did. By fourth grade, I was
back to being a girl, but I did continue to play on the soccer team.

And now to your son and your family.

1. First, I advise an honest look at yourself: your image of
   your gender and your attitudes, as well as those of your
   partner and your extended family. Is this going to be a huge
   challenge? An embarrassment? A contentious issue between
   generations? I don't have a magic trick for fixing this if it
   needs fixing. I believe that just laying it out in the open
   will be very helpful and, perhaps, the start of an important

emotional journey.

2. Now work on separating your and your family's attitudes from the reality of your son's sense of his identity. At the same time, I hope you'll acknowledge contemporary sensibilities, and heed the advice of child development professionals on meeting your child where he is and affirming that how he feels is how it is, at least for now, and it's okay.

3. Read about gender identity (on reputable sites: see below*) and discuss it further if needed with your child's pediatrician and teachers.

4. Understand that gender identity is powerful but also flexible and evolving. Most kids reach age four with an already deeply ingrained sense of being a girl or a boy, even when surrounded by models of very egalitarian and fluid gender roles and behaviors, even with and same-sex parents. But some reach this age with a different sense of self. Some kids are already quite firm in understanding themselves as other than the gender assumed to result from their sex. Thus, a girl may be very clear that she feels like a boy and vice versa. But other non-gender-conforming kids have a different sense about themselves: they may see themselves as a bit of both (e.g., a boy who wants to wear dresses *and* only play with boys) a neither/nor, or a question mark: for themselves, their parents, and society.

5. Start by affirming for your son that he is "the boss of his body and his feelings," and that you love him as he is, whatever way he feels about himself. At the same time, let him know that there is a wide range of feelings and behaviors that we associate with each gender, and they can change with time, or not, and either is okay.

6. Make a three-column list together with attributes and behaviors, asking him which is for the "boy" column, which for the "girl," and which for "both." This is your opportunity

to elicit his thoughts and also gently challenge rigid gender stereotypes. For example, some boys love ballet and are grand dancers, and girls can become firefighters (show him pictures or videos).

7. Look at the gender roles in your own family: is there room for a bit more fluidity and flexibility? It may be time to get yourself a tailored pantsuit and have your son and husband see *The Nutcracker*. Along these lines, look at your son's toys, room decorations, chores at home: everything may need a bit of a makeover to open up gender-stereotyping.

8. Note when other adults in your family and friends and colleagues fall back on traditional gender stereotypes (you'll be surprised how pervasive they are) and diplomatically comment to moderate both language and behavior.

9. Talk to your son about the specifics of what he wants to do to be a "boygle." Decide together which to implement now and which to put on hold. If some of the things on his list involve clear public manifestations, such as wearing a skirt or jewelry, you need to give him a realistic picture of how people will react. Start simple with: "If you want to wear a skirt, that's fine with me, but when we get on the bus, people will think you are a girl and speak to you like you are one." He may be fine with that. If so, ask him if he wants you to correct them and, if so, what to say, such as, for example: "He is a boy and he loves dressing up." If he decides he doesn't want that kind of attention, ask if he wants to wear skirts just at home, at least for now.

10. Ask how he wants to dress and play at his preschool and, once you have a clear sense of it, talk to the teachers about their response (there are many resources on what educational settings need to do to serve non-gender-conforming kids).

11. You may need to practice with him what *he* could say if someone is mean about it. If you're concerned about bullying,

read up about it now (don't put it off for too long), so you are prepared to address it.

12. Acknowledge that this may be very hard and up and down, as your son matures and either affirms this identity more and more or returns to a more conventional one, and get help from a therapist and/or child development specialist with expertise in this area.

13. Prepare for the long road ahead and embrace your son *as he is now*, staying open to changes as he gradually becomes the person he will be in adulthood.

* I recommend the resources offered by the American Academy of Pediatrics: https://pediatrics.aappublications.org/content/142/4/e20182162. A more user-friendly digest of the same information (by the same author, Dr. Jason Rafferty): https://www.healthychildren.org/English/ages-stages/gradeschool/Pages/Parenting-a-Gender-Diverse-Child-Hard-Questions-Answered.aspx

III. Preschool, Play, and the Big Wide World

Starting Preschool: Separation Difficulties

My son just started preschool two weeks ago, and he hangs on to me anywhere he can grab something and won't let go: my sleeve, my purse, my jacket. One day he wrapped his arms around my leg and wouldn't let go. He cries, "Mommy, don't go!" and it's all I can do not to bawl myself. The teachers assure me that minutes after I do leave, he is fine and joins the others in playing and circle time. What do I do?

Difficult separation at preschool (and kindergarten, too, even into first and second grade) is as common as the common cold and most frequently about as harmful. You are in good company with numerous other parents whose kids just started preschool or kindergarten. It might be reassuring to talk to other parents and hear if their kids are struggling too (though you court the danger of feeling like yours is the only one).

Here are some suggestions for easing separation at preschool or kindergarten:

1. *Accept* that crying is sometimes part of the process. Your goal is not to eliminate it in one fell swoop but to help your son overcome it so that he feels he's accomplishing something important on his own.

2. Give your son *something special that soothes him* to take to class with him. It can be a small stuffed animal, a family photo, a particular toy car, etc., that stays in his backpack. If he needs it closer by, put it in a fanny pack that he wears all day (at least initially).

3. Break the separation process into five simple steps and go through them fairly quickly:
   - Come in and greet the teachers
   - Put his backpack/lunchbox in his cubby
   - Pick a story to read or activity for him to do right after you leave
   - Have him walk you to the door and push you out, saying, "Bye, bye, mommy!" Shaking a maraca or tambourine at the same time helps, too.
   - Then he's to sit with a teacher for comforting. If needed, your son can dictate to the teacher a short letter to you about how he was sad when you left.

It helps to rehearse those steps at home once or twice soon after you get back from preschool, but not close to bedtime when you might hear some anxiety about going to school the next day. If you do, be reassuring and say: "Mommy will help you." Don't dwell on it.

Additional steps:

1. Leave a note in your son's lunchbox with words of encouragement and a photo of you/your family.

2. Tell your son when you'll pick him up: not by the time of day, but by the activity, e.g., "after afternoon circle time." Go over the sequences of activities until that point. If your son is having a very hard time, it's a good idea to have a shorter day for the first week or two. Come to pick him up after only

two or three activities. Say: "You'll have circle time, outside play, and snack, and then Mommy will come back: right after snack time."

3. If possible, get your son to pick in advance which teacher he wants to go to for comforting. This requires coordination with the preschool (as does, of course, the whole enterprise).

4. Work with the teachers to make sure they help your son verbalize being sad and, together, come up with something to do to help him feel better. They should not just distract him and gloss over the sadness.

5. Ask the teachers to text/email you about fifteen minutes after you've left to tell you how your son is doing.

6. Remember that when you pick up your son, you are there *for him*. Figure out getting the update from teachers earlier or later, so it doesn't interfere with reconnecting with your son.

It can take anywhere from a couple of weeks to a month, or even longer, for a child to feel fully comfortable separating from a parent. During that period, try to go easy on other separation situations (babysitters, staying with grandma). Remember, this is a precious learning opportunity: separation will keep coming throughout life. Mastered well now, it will become an important tool for many occasions in the future.

Free Play

My three-and-a-half-year-old daughter loves to play all kinds of board games and pretend games, do puzzles, and read books. But she generally insists that I play with her and looks to me to make up the games, either with set rules or as we go along. She also loves her enrichment classes: dance, Kindergym, and music. But I wonder if and when she needs to start playing on her own. I also hear and read about the importance of "free play," but I'm not exactly sure what that means and why it's so important.

Let me start with the good news: it sounds like you are spending a lot of time with your daughter playing together which fosters her emotional connection to you, her social and negotiating skills, her imagination, and, of course, her language, motor skills development, and ability to have fun. And I haven't heard anything about playing on a computer or other screen-based games (including those advertised as "educational"). While I'm not a purist on screen time (see the chapter on this topic) because sometimes a parent needs a break… the younger the child, the less time they should be playing using a screen.

And, yes, "free play" is a vital part of child development and is a bit different from what you're describing. The key feature of free play is that it is initiated by the child and springs from their imagination. At a young age, as a toddler, it may be simply pushing, stacking, and scattering blocks or toy cars, putting hats on and off, or rolling a ball. But full-fledged free play depends on two key factors that go hand-in-hand: language development and the ability to pretend.

Pretending is a fairly complex process where your child understands that she can conjure in her words a reality that is not actually unfolding in front of her. She can play going to the doctor or blast off to the moon. She can play pretend school, making herself the teacher and her stuffed animals the students. And when you can devote the time, attention, and patience, *you* can be among those students.

The reason this form of play is so important is it develops your child's imagination and inner life, as well as her ability to solve problems and work through her emotions. Often such free play is based on replicating situations and challenges from her life experience, such as being scared of the dentist, enacting learning and discipline in school, or working out fantasies of super-powers.

You can encourage free play by providing basic props: a simple doctor's kit, an empty cardboard box as a space ship, building blocks to build a castle where a drama involving a princess and her entourage is about to unfold. Simple props are better than elaborate ones because they leave more room for the imagination. However, as your child matures, she'll want more realistic ones, and that's perfectly fine.

Free play offers fertile ground for working out emotional issues. You'll see aggression worked on when dolls and super-powered characters go at each other. You'll see your child figuring out gender roles (more on that in a special chapter) with dress-up clothes and toy tools. You'll observe working out competitiveness and dealing with frustration when your child plays school. You'll note fears about body integrity in going to the doctor, dentist, and hairdresser games. And you'll get to see sibling rivalry, attachment and separation (and other family dynamics) when your child says, "Let's play family."

In all those situations, you can be a partial participant, helping to get things started and playing the role assigned to you by your child. But don't overdo it. Hang back a bit. Let your child run the show and use her own resources to develop the plot and solve problems. And remember that kids running their own game can be bossy and change the rules as they go to fit their vision of the game.

Kids don't need to be taught to engage in free play; it comes naturally to them. But they do need you to structure their day so that there is time for the unhurried, sometimes almost dreamy quality of enacting what's in their head. The biggest enemy of free play is daily life. It has too many structured activities and too easily available passive engagement and entertainment, such as watching TV of videos and screen-based education games, even you reading books to your child.

As your child gets older, you will likely encounter the "I am bored!" whine. Don't jump too fast to suggest an activity (even if it doesn't involve screens): boredom is often the starting point for truly imaginative, creative play. Being alone in one's head is essential to developing an inner life, and it starts early on.

If complaints of boredom persist, set up a "treasure box" of odds and ends: small toys, paper and pens, stickers, discarded knickknacks, a few dress-up items. Stash it in a closet or under a bed and pull it out when your child is bored. Let her explore the treasure box and come up with something to do. You can encourage her by saying, "Do/make/come up with something that will surprise me." Then sit back and wait. Soon you'll enjoy your child's creativity and, if you are lucky, eavesdrop a little on her chatter as she plays: you might hear some things she has worked out about the world that will amaze you.

Playdates

When is it time to start arranging playdates for my daughter? When is the right time to plan on leaving her at a friend's house without me present? Furthermore, if her friends want to come over for a playdate, up to what age (or developmental stage) do I make it mandatory that the parent remain present?

Playdates are a crucial part of social and emotional development in the preschool years and, of course, onward at school age. Of course, parents can get together with infants and toddlers and have them be together side by side and gradually learn to play together, but those are parent-led and supervised. Here I'll focus on playdates that lead to kids playing together independently.

The parameters for when and how depend on many factors, so I don't have a cookie-cutter answer. Let's begin with a quick, if fairly obvious, summary of why playdates are important:

1. Playing one-on-one with a friend is a basic building block of developing friendships, learning to share, take turns, negotiate and, when appropriate, hold your ground or ask for an adult's help.

2. Playdates at a friend's house are practice sessions in the separation process, as your child progresses from complete dependence on you to independence and self-confidence.

3. Playdates expose kids to the fact that not everyone is the same. Other families and homes have different environments,

rules, and family member constellations. A playdate may be your child's first exposure to differences in class and wealth, diverse ethnic and cultural traditions, variant behavior norms, same-sex couples, blended families—the list goes on.

4. Playdates allow your child to practice good manners and cooperation. Kids are generally on better behavior as guests at someone else's house than at home. Your child gets a chance to shine, and perhaps you'll see her in a more glowing light. If your child misbehaves on a playdate, take it as a warning sign that requires further examination: regarding either her sense of security and competence or the safety and age-appropriateness of rules and exposure at the host's home.

Now, here's a rather long list of what to consider when evaluating your child's readiness for playdates:

1. Is your child in a daycare/preschool where she's accustomed to playing with other kids for long stretches? If so, start a playdate with a friend from daycare.
2. Do you have neighbors or close friends with kids your child plays with often? If so, that's another option for starting playdates.
3. Is your child verbally developed enough to express her needs to the adult in the room if she's hurt (physically or emotionally), needs to go to the bathroom, or wants to go home? If she is but is very shy, is she emotionally developed enough to do so?
4. Is your child toilet-trained, and does she already have experience using bathrooms away from home and daycare?
5. Is your child still struggling with separation (from you and your partner at drop daycare drop off or when a babysitter comes)?
6. Is your child able to share, take turns, and negotiate without becoming aggressive?

If you've considered all these issues and feel your child is ready and, of course, your child *wants* a playdate, it's time. I recommend starting with a very familiar friend in your own home. If you know a somewhat older girl who likes your daughter and would come over for a playdate, that would be best. She would be the perfect teacher.

Before the friend comes over, go over the basic rules for a playdate:

1. You have to share your toys.
2. If there is something you don't want to share, that's okay, but you need to put it out of sight.
3. You take turns with your friend, and since your friend is a guest, they get to go first.
4. Your friend is the one who decides when she wants to go home (or it's prearranged with her parents). We generally don't ask our guests to leave. However, if there is a problem, ask a parent to help out.
5. We thank our friends for coming to our home when the playdate is over.

And consider these suggestions:

1. Sometimes it helps if the friend brings over some of her toys to play with—it makes it easier to share.
2. Prepare a snack in advance, and have your daughter serve it as a tea party.

After one or two playdates at your home, your child should, hopefully, be ready for a playdate at a friend's house. You (or another adult family member) need to be present for the entirety of the first few playdates. This makes your child feel secure., but it also lets you make sure she behaves appropriately and lets you watch the interactions—between children, the parent or parents, and the environment—to make sure you feel comfortable with all of those. If you don't, it can be rather awkward, but you need to find a diplomatic way of saying your child is not ready for playdates without you present. If the home is unacceptable (in terms of safety and adults' behavior), you'll have to bite the bullet and tell the parents you won't send your child there. Hard... but sometimes necessary.

If a child comes over and behaves unacceptably, you have a similarly difficult situation. I suggest taking the bull by the horns and telling the parent or parents about those behaviors. You can certainly try to soften it by saying, "Maybe the rules at our home are rather stricter than yours," or "Maybe your child is not quite ready to come over without you." It isn't easy.

Your child is ready for playdates without you when you are confident she'll behave appropriately, she has little trouble separating, and she says she wants it. Plan to go over a few "what ifs" in preparation: "What will you do if you need to go to the bathroom? If your friend is mean to you? If you don't like the snack his mom gives you?" Satisfied your child is ready, start with a short playdate, where you are away for no more than an hour. Most kids over age three-and-half build up quickly to playdates of two to three hours with good friends and trusted adults. That would give you a nice window to relax or do errands. Remember that starting with a short playdate with no tears is far better than a long one with them. And be sure to reciprocate!

Selective Mutism: My Daughter Won't Talk at Preschool, But at Home, She's a Chatterbox

My daughter started preschool at the beginning of September and seemed to adjust well. She goes to school without any fuss and looks happy when I pick her up. She tells me what she did at school and says she likes it. But I just got a note from her teacher: she has not said a single word since school started! She neither speaks up on her own initiative nor answers the teachers' direct questions. It's been six weeks and zero words. But otherwise, she is cooperative and seems to follow what's going on in class.

Should I be alarmed? At home, she talks plenty: to my husband and me, to our dog, and to her dolls. The only information I can add is she is shy both with strangers (probably a good thing) and with our extended family members, all of whom live far away, so she sees them only once or twice a year.

It is rare that I tell a parent to worry more than they already do. The vast majority of parents have an overstock of "ready-to-worry" items in their psychic wardrobe. It's a bit like the classic *Jewish Telegram* (or nowadays, *Jewish Tweet)*: "Start worrying. Details to follow." But this time I do want to raise your anxiety. It's in service of helping your daughter as early as possible on the chance that this is not a passing phase.

What you describe may be the telltale signs of selective mutism, a childhood disorder affecting one to two percent of children across all cultures. It's twice as common in girls as in boys. The frequency doubles in bilingual families and recent immigrants. The onset is typically at ages two-and-a half to three-and-a-half, most often in a child's first daycare or preschool setting.

Selective mutism (hereafter SM) is associated with other forms of anxiety (especially social anxiety) on either parent's side. Treatment, when started early, is very effective; the sooner, the better. But it does take time, a carefully crafted behavioral intervention, and close collaboration between home, school, and the treating team.

The treatment team should include a behavioral specialist, a speech and language therapist, and a pediatric psychiatrist. They should be assessing the situation, and in severe cases, possibly prescribing anti-anxiety medication. It usually requires at least several months of treatment, if not most of her first school year. More limited intervention may be needed at the start of the next grade or when entering other group settings.

Now that I have alarmed you, hopefully into taking measured actions rather than freaking out, let me reassure you a bit.

1. This could, indeed, be just a temporary adjustment phase. That said, please don't wait much longer to see if it resolves on its own.
2. Pressing or encouraging your child to talk in school is usually counterproductive.

3. It is *essential* to have a correct diagnosis. Some children presenting this way are suffering from a different condition, such as extreme shyness. (Kids who have SM may, in fact, not be shy. They can be outgoing and socially active, but nonverbally so.) It could also be hearing impairment, speech/language development problems, depression, or social anxiety.

4. Some kids with SM have extreme sensory sensitivity. All or some everyday sensory stimulation (sound, sight, touch, taste, smell) overwhelms them. What seems like ordinary street noise or physical contact to you is bombardment to them. For them, SM is a coping mechanism for shutting out the onslaught of stimulation.

5. Some kids are extremely slow to warm up. What takes average children a few days or two weeks can take them months. This would be a pattern you see in multiple settings: adjusting to new people or places, changed daily routines, even new clothes or shoes.

6. There are excellent resources for information, referrals, and state-supported diagnostic and treatment services (check with your pediatrician for your locale), and parent-to-parent support. I'll cite only three here: these are your gateways to everything you might need:
   - The Selective Mutism Foundation: https://www.selectivemutismfoundation.org/;
   - The Diagnostic Center of Northern California: www.dcs-cde.ca.gov/
   - The Selective Mutism Group: http://www.selectivemutism.org/ (parents' resources & support network)

Start by gathering information. If, by the time you feel well informed about SM and all the services available to you, the problem has gone away, that's very fortunate. If not, you have a long road ahead of you. Don't delay getting started.

Going to the Doctor, Dentist, and Hairdresser

My three-year-old son seems awfully worried about going to the doctor and the dentist. He also refuses to get a haircut and says he's scared. I have been contemplating cutting the bangs that already hang over his eyes (and annoy him to no end) while he's asleep, but I'm worried it'll freak him out even more. Perhaps I could forget about the haircut for a while, but he does need to go to the doctor and dentist for his regular checkups and, when he does get sick, I don't want it to be such an ordeal (for him and me). Why is he so scared, and how can I help him?

It may seem obvious why kids are scared of the doctor: they get shots there! Those shots hurt and may also, in a young child's mind, get mixed up with things he's overheard about people getting shot. You'd wish not, but often we can't protect our kids as much as we'd like to. The dentist's visit should, hopefully, not hurt (keep those candies to a minimum), but it's pretty weird and can be uncomfortable.

The hairdresser may be a bit harder to understand, but the fact is, many if not most young children (between two and five) are, at least for a while, afraid. I think it's that their sense of the wholeness of their body (so-called "body integrity") is still evolving. Even though they know that getting their hair cut doesn't hurt (and you can show this with a small snip of your hair and then your child's), it's still spooky to them, like losing a part of their bodies. This returns when they start losing their teeth, hence the need to mollify them with the Tooth Fairy. Therefore, a lot of young children are both scared of and mesmerized by haircuts and often try to give themselves a haircut on the sly.

These reactions are of a piece with the general phenomenon you may have observed where a minor bruise or tiny scrape or cut generates an extreme reaction. Even if barely visible, it absolutely requires major intervention, namely a Band-Aid, preferably a huge one or several with pictures on them, to keep on the boo-boo in question... forever.

So, once you have understood why it's such a big deal for your child, you can appreciate the following suggestions:

1. Play out the anticipated appointment at home: doctor, dentist, or hairdresser, for a day or two. Let your child play both the patient *and* the doctor, the client *and* the hairstylist.
2. Doctors' and dentists' kits are excellent tools for practicing, and you can make your own hairdresser's kit from what you have at home.
3. Badges of honor (stickers) and small treats are definitely in order. Make sure your doctor/dentist/hairdresser has them (Is there a doctor's office anywhere that does not give out lollipops?).
4. Read books about these experiences ahead of the appointment and afterward, as well. Some TV shows can help, too, such as relevant *Daniel Tiger* episodes.
5. If your child is very scared, especially of the doctor, you may want to go for a visit without an actual appointment. The visit is to spend some time in the doctor's office (most have toys and books), talk to the nurses, chat with the doctor for a moment to say hello, maybe get on the scale, but without any procedures. It will reassure your child that the doctor is a nice person and will take good care of him.
6. After the appointment, talk about it to mom, older siblings, grandparents, and let your child describe how he managed. Avoid an exaggerated "Jon was SO BRAVE!" Whatever he says, even if he says he was scared and cried, gives him more of a feeling of mastery than your praise.

All of this said, don't overdo the preparations. A day or two before the appointment is plenty of time to address the anxiety and try to help your child get through it.

Talking to Strangers

Is talking to strangers still a big "no-no?" My daughter is extremely outgoing and loves to chat people up in line at the supermarket, at a nearby table in the café, and walking down the street. I hate to bridle her enthusiasm and hate even more to make her afraid. Is it really necessary? After all, she's never without a trusted adult supervising, and I don't anticipate she will ever go back to the "good old days" and walk home from school on her own. But... of course, I worry that I am not protecting her enough. What do you think?

I and, most likely, you as well certainly remember the "stranger danger" panic of nearly two decades ago. I thought then that it was extreme, too scary for kids, and ineffectual. I still think so now. Here's why:

1. First of all, the young children it was supposed to inoculate against marauding strangers (it was aimed at kids from age four and up) cannot exercise the judgment and self-control needed to implement the lessons of "stranger danger" training. In actual situations where a stranger offers them candy, chocolate, or anything of that sort, they would follow their mouth and stomach, not the recited lines.

2. The idea that strangers are dangerous is too frightening for young kids. After all, they are often surrounded by strangers when out in public: are they supposed to be scared of all of them? Furthermore, the nature of the danger is not comprehensible to children under age six or seven, so teaching them about it is scaring them—as noted above—to no useful end.

3. The panic about stranger abduction was, to a great degree, a distraction from the fact that the overwhelming majority of unauthorized contacts ("abduction" at the far end of the spectrum) are by adults who are family members or friends/ neighbors, not strangers.

4. Talking to strangers is, in fact, something we adults often do as part of normal social interactions. Telling young children never to do it while they see us doing it regularly is confusing, at best.

5.   Most of us now structure our children's lives so that they are never left unsupervised. They are always watched over by a trusted adult, be it us, a family member, teacher, babysitter, sports coach, or someone else. Gone are the days of children under age ten taking buses by themselves or walking alone to and from school. By the time your child is mature enough to be alone (or with just her friends) in public, she will have understood how to behave toward strangers. The real danger from strangers is now mostly on the internet. That is something you need to discuss with your child at length and repeatedly, once you allow her to surf the web on her own.

Thus, I recommend avoiding any of the "stranger danger" teachings, songs, memes, and so on. Your child will learn how to interact appropriately and safely with strangers by merely observing you as you go about your daily life. Meanwhile, let her chat up the person behind you at the store checkout, say hi to a security guard stationed outside a bank, and greet the mailman with a big smile. *They* will all appreciate it.

"What Happened to Your Legs?": Kids Reacting to Visible Disabilities

I was walking down the street with my four-year-old son. As we approached a man in a wheelchair, my son called out at the top of his voice (and, let me tell you, he can project!) "Mommy, what's wrong with the man's legs?" I was so embarrassed! I pulled him to my side (Okay, I yanked his arm a bit) and said: "Shush, don't say that!" The man in the wheelchair turned his chair around and hurried away from us.

I know I didn't react well, but what should I have said? What's an appropriate response in this instance and, more generally, when kids ask bluntly about people with (visible) disabilities?

To write this chapter, I consulted with my friend Jim, who was born with spina bifida and has been a wheelchair user since he was a toddler (you can now see him in his incredible documentary, *Crip Camp*, part of the Obamas' *Higher Ground* series on Netflix). He's heard it all: "What happened to you? Why don't you have regular legs? Can I ride in your wheelchair? Lucky you, you can ride," and more. Some kids even ask if he was *born* in a wheelchair; he answers: "Don't you think that would be a bit painful for my mom?"

Still, he'd take a socially inappropriate question, especially from a child, any day over the more common responses: yanking the child away, averting one's eyes, or looking past him as if he's not there.

To be honest, your reaction was, indeed, unfortunate. But you can repair the damage. Start by talking it over at home and answering your son's questions. Then, next time you encounter someone in a wheelchair, model for your son by starting a typical friendly conversation with a stranger, e.g., "Beautiful day to be out, isn't it?" As the conversation unfolds, you can introduce your son. You may open by asking, "Is it okay if my son asks you some questions? He is curious." If the person agrees, encourage your child to ask any questions he may have.

Children are naturally curious about people who look different than the ordinary; sometimes, they are not only puzzled but even frightened. There's nothing wrong with their innocent questions, as long as you require the same good manners you expect in conversation with any adult. On the contrary, it's a great opportunity to teach your child not to stigmatize anyone different from them, be it by visible disabilities, skin color, social or intellectual abilities, or foreign accents. It also allows you to check your automatic, unconscious reactions to disabilities. Do you need to work on yourself first?

Thus, when you next encounter someone in a wheelchair, you might suggest to your child asking, "Excuse me, sir, can I ask you something about your wheelchair?" Encourage a simple inquiry such as: "Why do you have to be in a wheelchair" but don't shush, yank away, or censor less polite ones such as, "What's wrong with your legs?" Most likely, you'll get a simple answer, such as "I was born this way," or "My legs don't work well enough for walking." I hope (and bet) that you'll get more: elaborations, such as "But I can drive a car, and I have a really interesting job doing ___. And I love chocolate, don't you?"

From here, let the conversation flow naturally. Your child might want to know how the person can drive a car, what kind of job they have, what else they can do in the wheelchair. You'll have accomplished the key lesson: the person with a disability has one area of their life that may be more challenging than what you face, but they are a full person with a rich, active life, not a fixture in a wheelchair.

Often, young kids will be curious about the wheelchair itself. They may want to try operating it or going for a ride. Jim usually turns his power chair off when an interested child engages him. He then asks the parent if it's okay to show their child how the chair works and lets them try the joystick control (which may be familiar from video games). Then, after confirming with the parent again, Jim may allow the child to maneuver the chair on the lowest speed and, if the kid is small enough and the parent agrees, take him for a short ride on the sidewalk.

This experience will then be an excellent opening for further discussion at home of disabilities, both visible and hidden, and other physical differences. Ask your child about his school: is there anyone there who has special challenges? Is there anyone in your family? In your neighborhood? If the answer to all three is "no," you should either get out more or expose your child to the issues through books and other media.

Oy Vey: My Son Wants a Gun!

We thought we'd skirted the issue with our pro-peace, "use your words," and gender-neutral parenting, but alas, our four-year-old boy has sniffed it somewhere: he wants a gun. We cringe at the thought but can also see that he has never wanted anything else with this kind of intensity. Help!

Let's start with assuring you that you have done nothing wrong in raising your boy in the "paths of peace," and his wish for a gun now does not indicate he will want one when he is grown. This issue is particularly fascinating to me because of its gender and cultural specificity, so bear with me for some broad discussion before we get into what to do.

Gender: I advise parents to offer a full spectrum of toys and activities without gender-pegging (as I did with my children): boys with dolls, girls with hammers, and so on. I have never encountered parents flummoxed because their daughter wanted a gun. I, myself, remember vividly how I insisted on playing soccer with the boys and wanted a bow and arrow for the Jewish holiday of Lag Ba'Omer. My father was a carpenter and physicist (in those days on the kibbutz, you could be both), so he made me a beautifully carved bow and explained the laws of physics governing the arrow's trajectory and speed. I even announced in third grade that my name was now Danny and that I was going to be a boy. It lasted until the start of fourth grade. But never, in that whole period, nor before or after, did I want a gun.

Which brings me to the second point:

Culture: My kibbutz was on the Jordanian border, and guns, carried by the watchmen and soldiers, were part of everyday life. It is still the case in Israel today: you see soldiers on their way to and from home, and other security personnel carry guns everywhere. Yet deaths and injury from gun violence (outside army operations— not within the scope of this book) are unheard of. When it came to raising my children here in the United States, I, too, felt very uncomfortable with the idea of my son playing with guns. So, what do I recommend?

I do believe boys love toy guns so much because they offer an important avenue for mastering aggression through play. Combative pretend play—such as Cowboys and Indians, Space Aliens and Humans, Cops and Robbers, and Superheroes—is important for the maturation and "civilizing" of boys. Often, in those games, the boys visualize being armed to the teeth. Opportunities for play that channels aggressive fantasies may, ultimately, reduce the amount of actual aggression toward other kids.

That said, it's important to uphold your values and recognize when something is too uncomfortable and disturbing for you (as I said, I'm with you on this). It's perfectly fine to let your child know there are things you find objectionable and don't want in your house (some feel this way about pet rats). We told our son: "We really, really don't like guns. They hurt and kill people. We don't want one in our house, not even a play gun."

But we did let him get a plastic sword. Why? Mainly because it didn't make us cringe in the same way a gun did and let him deal with aggression through play. We explained: "Swords are a bit like old tales from 'Once upon a time.' A long, long time ago, people used them to fight. But, nowadays, people don't use swords to kill." No doubt, there is a bit of rationalizing here, but this offered a middle ground we could live with. Our son, after graduating from swords to the World Wrestling Federation, abandoned these pursuits and has grown up to be a very peaceful, unaggressive person, who does his "fighting" for justice and civil rights in the court of law.

Where's your comfort zone? Maybe you'll go with the "sword solution," or maybe you'll allow water pistols but not realistic-looking guns. Know that if you ban guns altogether, your son will make them with his hand, a bent twig, a discarded door handle. But that's creativity: let it be!

At an opportune moment, when he is older, I hope you'll have a serious talk about the scourge of guns.

Generosity

I'm a teacher at a Jewish preschool where Friday mornings begin with passing around the tzedakah *(charity) box. One boy in my class held onto his pennies tightly when the tzedakah box reached him and would not put them in. "I need the money for college!" he explained. The other children were shocked. My co-teacher said to him sweetly that she was sure he would change his mind soon, but he continued to insist he had to keep those pennies. Was there another way to handle this? And, more broadly, how do we encourage the development of generosity in young children?*

This is a perfect illustration of the complexity of teaching and modeling altruism to young children! Let's parse it into three core components:

1. The value of money
2. Child-to-child generosity
3. Generalized altruism toward "those in the world who need our help."

The Value of Money: You could see from the child's insistence that the money was for his college fund that he hears discussions of money and saving at home, but, of course, has no concept of real finances (five cents vs. the cost of college). Young children only begin to grasp the value of money (up to $10–$20) at school-age and of larger amounts, certainly college costs, only in their teens. Teaching the value of spending wisely and saving is important but only effective through parents' long-term modeling.

Preschoolers understand that the shiny copper and silver disks have some kind of magic power, but that's about it. If you really want them to understand saving for the future, start with concrete things, such as "Let's save half the cupcake for the afternoon," or "How about saving some Play-Dough for tomorrow?"

Child-to-Child Generosity: The "Nature vs. Nurture" debate about the development of altruism in children is a hot topic, requiring more room than we have here. Jean Piaget (old news, but still valuable) held that only in the last "formal operational stage" (age eleven to sixteen and up), with the development of abstract reasoning, could a child comprehend altruism and autonomously act on it. Newer research has identified "spontaneous altruism" in toddlers, chimpanzees, and... rats. For now, suffice it to say that many researchers today believe there is a strong innate altruism, balanced by healthy egocentrism, observable already in toddlers' behavior.

All this pertains to the immediate world of the child—family and peers—and this is the altruism to foster now. Thus, if another child offers his extra pennies, rather than telling that boy what a nice thing he had done, I'd ask his peers what they thought. Their appreciation would go much further in inculcating the emotional rewards of generosity. Because money is so abstract, the best ways to encourage child-to-child altruism are through giving and sharing of "real" things like toys, treats, or a teacher's lap (suggestions: https://www.apa.org/monitor/dec06/kids).

General Altruism: Altruism toward anonymous people in the world who need our help requires abstract thinking: the ability to imagine and care about people you don't know and haven't even seen. It also depends on the full comprehension of the value of money. As I said, preschoolers possess neither. So, have your preschool "adopt" an organization that serves people or animals in your own community: a homeless shelter, animal rescue, or local park. Consider that kids relate more easily to abandoned animals than to more abstract "poor people." Get the kids collecting toys, books, clothes, and pet treats or planting flowers. They understand the value of these from their own daily experiences.

I know this leaves the tzedakah box out of the picture, and you do want to teach the Jewish practice of tzedakah. Keep the tzedakah box out, but realize it provides learning by imitation and rote, not by deep experience. To teach altruism to preschoolers, think "out of the box."

Getting Ready for Kindergarten

Our daughter starts kindergarten in a month and already shows signs of anxiety. She keeps saying, "Kindergarten will be fun, right?" and has been clingy. Can we help her get ready?

Now is the perfect time to start preparing for kindergarten. Some five-year-olds, especially firstborns, find going to kindergarten as baffling as going to Mars. Everybody talks about it and asks them if they are excited, but they have no idea what it really is and how to get there. Many parents navigate this passage with baggage—happy or unhappy memories and the realization that "your baby" is no baby anymore, making it more fraught.

Kids who attend preschool may find the transition easy. Simply say: "Kindergarten is like preschool for older children. You do a lot of the same things: circle time, playing, learning things. You also learn to read and write." Make sure she understands that learning to read and write takes a long time. Many kids come home from the first day of kindergarten crestfallen: "But I don't know how to read yet!" Add relevant information such as larger class size (alas... budget cuts), the greater variety of kids (ethnically, ability levels), and addressing the teacher more formally.

If your child is new to group care, allow more time and effort to prepare her (suggestions follow). Whether she is a seasoned preschooler or new to group care, this preparation depends first and foremost on her temperament. If your child is shy, slow to warm up, struggles with changes and transitions, she'll need more preparation and support.

You need information about your child's kindergarten to prepare. I'll assume that, like most parents I know, you have done a thorough investigation, so you have the necessary details. Your key steps are:

Visit the classroom the week before school starts when the teacher is present, setting up (most schools welcome this). Introduce your child to the teacher, the room, and the daily routine. Make sure to show her where the bathroom is and have the teacher explain how bathroom breaks will work.

When visiting, find out the plan for the first day of kindergarten. If it will be the usual—parents stay for the first period and then leave—let your child know. Tell her, "I'll be back to pick you up after lunch/afternoon snack [whatever fits]."

Be prepared for a surprisingly intense wave of emotions for you when you leave her there. Your child will hopefully not cry, but you may! I suggest a tissue pack and coffee with a friend.

In many schools, kids line up in the yard before going into the classes. During your visit, ask about it. Explain how it will work and point out to your child where to line up in the yard and let her explore the play structures.

Play "kindergarten" at home. Your child plays the teacher, and you (or her sibling or friend) are the student. Let her practice typical kindergarten routines. Be sure to listen for unrealistic expectations/worries and correct them.

If you know any future classmates, arrange playdates before school starts.

Many kids somehow gather that you're supposed to cry on the first day of kindergarten. Let your child know it's not required. Tell her some kids do cry because they may not be used to being in school, away from their parents, or get so excited they burst into tears.

Buy a backpack and a few school supplies in advance, letting her pick what she wants (within reason). Pre-pack it with a laminated family photo and a note from you. If she has a "lovie," let her take it in the backpack for the first week.

Make a "My Kindergarten Book" together. Page 1: current photo of your child. Page 2: family photo. Page 3: photos of the school building, the class, and the teacher (from the school's website or your visit). On Page 4, your child draws and dictates her expectations before school starts. Once school starts, do a page per day until your child loses interest.

Prepare, but don't obsess. On the first day, remember to bring tissues and a camera (if you still have this antiquated gadget. It's better than your iPhone, which is likely to distract you from the important moment you are witnessing).

PART III:
The Elementary School Years

1. Family and Friends Behavior and Relationships

Nightmares and Scary TV Programs

*O*ur six-year-old son just started having significant anxiety at bedtime, requiring my husband or me to stay with him until he falls asleep (not easy since we also have to put our three-year-old to bed at the same time). It used to be that when he was anxious about the dark at bedtime, our cat would sleep in his room, and that would soothe him. But he says the cat no longer works. When we sit with him, he falls asleep very, very quickly, so it hasn't been an impossible ordeal. But for three nights in a row now, he's been waking up in the middle of the night and demanding, almost hysterically, that we sleep in his room all night. He says he is afraid that worms will come out of his nose, something he saw on Clone Wars, his favorite TV show.

1. For now, how do we deal with this bedtime and middle-of-the-night?

2. *For the longer term, what should be our TV policy?* Clone Wars *is his favorite show, and there might be WWIII if we take it away. Maybe we should anyway. But more importantly, should we be dramatically changing our threshold for what constitutes suitable screen time?*

Scary TV programs… boys (and some girls, too) love them and get freaked out by them. What are parents to do?

At Night

Your son needs you when he is this frightened. I recommend you sleep in his room for a few nights to relieve his fear. It should take four to five nights to get him back to sleeping through. Knowing you'll be in his room all night will also help him fall asleep more easily at bedtime. Right now, he is afraid to let himself fall asleep, worrying he'll have nightmares about the worms and other scary things that tag along with them.

After the night-waking stops, praise him for his victory. Make a "Certificate of Accomplishment for Winning the War Against the Scary Worms from TV" (buy a gold-lettered one in a stationery store, or download from the internet). Assure him that you'll come to him if he needs you in the middle of the night. Leave your camping mattress in his room for a while, a visual reminder that you'll be there when he's scared.

Daytime

It's important to help your son get the frightening images "out of his system" first. Even though he may be reluctant because "it's too scary," get him to draw the worms. Then suggest he cross them out with a thick black marker or tear up the picture. Let him make play-dough worms, then bash them with his fist or stomp on them. Also, ask your pediatrician to call him or send him a letter on office stationery saying there is no such thing as worms coming out of kids' noses.

Now let's go back to how it started: Scary TV shows aimed at young boys. Oy! There are so many programs for young kids that are way too scary! It's also common for a child to happily watch a program for months, and, suddenly, get terrified by a single scene. As they mature, they become more aware of things that are truly frightening in the real world. Thus, scary TV scenes trigger fears, as if out of the blue. Remember that the things he is afraid of (worms in his nose, ghosts) are often not real, but *the fear itself certainly is!*

I am not well versed in the clones and their wars, but clearly, your son is showing you how much they scare him. Is he going to renounce watching the program? Probably not. Should you banish it from the house? Probably... at least for a while. However, given the "threat of WWIII," I understand your reluctance. If you are not going to ban the show, you should watch it with him. Better yet, record and preview it. Let him know in advance if there will be a scary scene and be ready with the remote so you can fast forward past it. However, playing out scenes and characters from the program with toy figures and dress-up is very valuable. It'll help your son conquer the scary images, develop his imagination and his ability to channel his own aggression into pretend play, and build his emotional vocabulary.

Now get some sleep!

Sleepovers

Our six-year-old daughter has been talking about sleepovers for two months now. It seems all her school friends (she's in first grade) have sleepovers every weekend, and Monday morning, it's all they can talk about. Our daughter has been invited many times—she is well-liked by her friends—but she always finds an excuse for why she can't go. I am beginning to suspect she has significant anxiety about it but doesn't feel comfortable "fessing up" to her friends, or even to us, her parents.

Is she missing an essential part of social-emotional development? Should we press her to tell us why she is reluctant? Encourage her to overcome her anxiety and go on sleepovers? Drop the whole thing until she brings it up? I don't want to be an alarmist... but I confess I wonder how she'll go away to college.

Let me begin with reassurance: she *will* go to college, and you won't have to sleep in her dorm room. But seriously, let's first clarify the function and value of sleepovers and then address the question of timing and how to support a reluctant child in venturing there.

Sleepovers have two major functions, which are kind of obvious, but still:

1. They are practice for separation from both home and parents and venturing into the bigger world. They are essential preparation for vacations away from home, sleep-away camp, and yes, eventually, college and adult life.
2. Sleepovers create a very special social-emotional space, where bonding with friends is deeper and where kids often first learn to share intimately.

Sleepovers are generally (at least in the US) uni-gender, so those for boys and girls often, but not always, have different qualities. Boys' sleepovers are often opportunities for horsing around, competitive feats of one kind or another, and comparing penis size and function (yes, it's an important part of growing up male). Girls tend to share much more about their intimate feelings: early on about family and friends and later about crushes (on either gender) and the trials and tribulations of puberty.

So, indeed, sleepovers are a key part of growing up in our culture. What, then, should you do about your child's avoidance of them? First, gently open up a conversation about it. If she can't explain why she's reluctant, offer some possibilities. They include (but are not limited to):

1. *Homebodyism:* Some kids (and adults) just don't like being away from home and their own bed. If you or someone else in your family is like that—point it out and normalize it.
2. *Sleep difficulties or mild separation anxiety:* If your child has a hard time falling asleep or still wakes in the middle

of the night and needs your reassurance, a sleepover is a scary thought. Again, normalize this by giving examples of someone similar that way. If none come to mind, turn to "The Princess and the Pea."

3. **Stronger separation anxiety:** A child who is unusually anxious about separation in general will find sleepovers frightening. This situation warrants additional consideration and possibly therapeutic intervention before you move ahead with sleepovers.

4. **Bedwetting:** Clearly, if your child still wets her bed on occasion (not uncommon up to age eight, more so for boys), avoiding sleepovers is pretty much a necessity.

5. **Social insecurity:** If a child is socially anxious and unusually worried about her friendships, a sleepover, with the implied intimacy and bonding, may be too worrying.

6. **Gender issues:** Sleepovers would likely be a problem for a child struggling with their gender identity (more in a sperate chapter on gender roles and identity).

Now that you've considered all these and ferreted out your child's situation and worries, what's the best course of action for her and your family? You can decide that together, though you might want to consult your pediatrician or a child therapist. Ruling out sleepovers, at least for now, is a perfectly acceptable choice. Your course of action is to either help your child with strategies to manage sleepovers *if* she *wants* to go on them or support your child to feel okay about the reason she won't do sleepovers now. If the reason is something she's embarrassed about, say bedwetting, help her formulate an explanation that protects her privacy. For example, the statement "I never sleep well not in my own bed. When my family goes on vacation, it takes me hours to fall asleep. My dad is the same way" is much less embarrassing.

If you've chosen to help your daughter overcome her reluctance and start going on sleepovers, here are some strategies for mastering sleepovers:

1. Practice!
   - Hold pretend sleepovers. Start at home, having your child sleep in a sleeping bag in a room other than her bedroom. It can be the living room, a balcony (weather permitting), or even—if you have it—a large walk-in closet.
   - If you are lucky and have friendly next-door neighbors, have a sleepover there. Grandparents, aunts and uncles, and beloved babysitters are also good options. Or do a sleepover together—your child and you (or an older sibling if you have one on hand)—at a friend's house.

2. Sleepovers without sleep: let your child go on a sleepover but plan on picking her up about half an hour after lights are out (coordinate with the hosting parents so that your child is near the door and easy to extricate quietly). Prepare a face-saving explanation such as "Our family has special plans early the next morning"—plan something so this is true.

3. Equip your child with security gadgets of various sorts, such as a lovely, a special blanket, a favorite book, earphones to plug into a phone or CD player so she can listen to a soothing recording, and, finally—and most importantly—a way to reach you if she needs you (phone).

4. Ask your child if she wants you to talk to the hosting parents and review what she'd like you to tell them about helping her if she's anxious.

5. For kids age eight and up, the hosts may be providing fairly minimal supervision, just making sure they and the house and furniture are safe (definitely check on this with the hosts in advance). So you may initiate a conversation about what topics the kids might be discussing. See if there is anything that makes your child feel uncomfortable. Stress/support that it's perfectly fine to say "I don't want to talk about this" or "I don't want to do this," especially as it pertains to private body parts. That said, you may want to normalize things and

say something like, "Oh, yes... boys this age like to show off their penises," or "You know, girls your age often like to whisper about the boys they like, but you don't have to either like someone that way or talk about it."

Take your time and let your child dictate the pace. If sleepovers are a challenge, the key is for you to support her in mastering them, not to do it for her— like most things in parenting.

Limit Setting: School-Age Kids

My five-and-a-half-year-old son is still a handful. Of course, he's much more reasonable than he was at age three (oh, the tantrums...), but getting him to follow rules and requests is still a challenge. Not a daily one, thank goodness, but on average, two or three times a week, we'll have a confrontation about something he is supposed to do (or NOT do). He has graduated to arguing and pouting and, sometimes, yelling instead of the tantrums he used to have. It's still exhausting and frustrating, as often I feel like I get drawn into arguing with him endlessly. It may start as a reasonable back-and-forth negotiation but quickly deteriorates into an angry power struggle and shouting match (most often his, but not always). Help!

Setting limits is a continuous task and carries into the school-age years. Often things will smooth out by age six or seven but then make a comeback, in spades, in adolescence. I'll focus here on the period of kindergarten through second grade, hoping to set you on a good course for now and later years.

Let's recap why children *need* limits, even if they give you a hard time while you're setting them:

1. To be and feel safe in the world around them
2. To help manage their own intense emotions, especially anger, that threaten to overwhelm them
3. To learn how to deal with frustration and anger using words, not aggression

4. To learn how to react when aggression comes at them from peers

5. To know they can always rely on their parents (and other care-taking adults) for their physical and emotional safety.

By this age, most kids have learned to manage their emotions most of the time. But there are still many moments of extremely intense emotional reactions when their skills and words fail them. They still need repetition and support, with the message "Your feelings are okay, whatever they are; what we expect you to manage is how you express them in your actions."

As awkward as it may seem, *writing down your rules* is still an excellent place to start. Have your child make his list of the family rules, while you make yours. Then compare the two and agree on the core rules by which everyone will abide. Fairness is key at this age: how many times have you heard a protest or whine, "But it's not *fair!*" Be sure that the rule "no yelling at each other" applies to both of you (and everyone else in the family).

Once you have your list of rules (including obligations, like completing household chores or homework before play, and prohibitions, like no screen time after 8:00 PM), lay out consequences for breaking the rules. Hopefully, these will be by mutual agreement, but remember you are the deciding authority, so you can impose consequences even if your son protests. Add positive consequences (aka "rewards") for complying with the rules. A simple way to do this is on a time axis: starting with a day at a time but moving toward a week at a time. A day/week with no rules broken earns your son something special, preferably a particular activity with you, the whole family, or a friend. Working toward earning something he wants is fine, too, with points for good days adding up to a reasonable target you set in advance. In this plan, a day with one transgression means not earning a point, but a day with two or more is an equivalent deduction of points.

It's important to agree, as part of your strategy, on a process of negotiations (aka "arguing") about rules and privileges. You want to avoid getting dragged into an endless argument that escalates into nagging, whining, or yelling. Negotiations, rather than arguing, involve these steps:

1. Your child makes his argument for what he wants.

2. You listen and don't answer immediately, but rather, take a few minutes (for big issues you may need to take a day and include discussion with your partner). If your son is very impatient (and you tend to be reactive), use a timer set for ten minutes.

3. Come back with your response: often offer a compromise but sometimes say "no."

4. Now your child has a chance for a rebuttal. Explain that he needs to add something new to his argument, not just repeat what he said at first. Listen attentively! If he makes a good argument, let him know. Tell him you appreciate how he's thinking about it and presenting his view and point out the most compelling part of his argument.

5. Take a bit more time to think about it, making it clear that badgering you with further arguments will automatically mean the answer will be "no."

If your child is very prone to arguing, it might help to start a game called "You Be the Judge." You present him with a dilemma (both ethical and practical, but don't make it too close to what you're dealing with at home), and *he* has to decide what should be done. This puts him in the parental position you're holding and will gradually develop his ability to see both sides of the coin in a variety of situations and understand how hard it is to be fair and just.

Finally, at certain times your child may still be so overwhelmed with frustration and anger that he throws a tantrum or acts aggressively. Unlike with very young children, where you need to stay close at hand and reassuring, you can tell your child the behavior is unacceptable and send him to his room to "blow off steam and calm down." If he's the kind of kid who lashes out physically, you can still try to hold him in an enveloping-restraining hug to contain him (only if you are strong enough so that it's safe for you). Otherwise, send him to his room, where he has pillows to punch; a bean bag to stomp, kick, and jump on; or a bop bag to pounce on and wrestle down. After the storm passes, have a quiet conversation about helping him to manage his rage. Consider enrolling him in a martial arts class or, if it's a persistent issue, in an appropriate therapy group.

Sometimes the exchange is so intense it sets you off, so you may feel like throwing a tantrum yourself, yelling at your child, or... even hitting. Losing your cool once in a while is a common part of parenting. If you do so with your child, be sure to address it:

1. Take your own time out. Say, "I need a little time out to calm down," and model by taking demonstrative deep breaths, counting out loud to 10, closing your eyes, putting on headphones to listen to music, or whatever works best.

2. Apologize if you yelled at him. Say something like: "I am so sorry I yelled at you. I was too angry when I did it, and I shouldn't have. It makes me feel bad/sad now. I'm sorry."

3. If you find that you lose it often, *you* need more help. Talk to a therapist, a child development specialist, your pediatrician, or a support group: you are not the only one!

Aggressive at Home

Since our daughter started kindergarten, she's become aggressive. When angry, tired, or hungry, she kicks, hits, scratches, and bites. But never at kindergarten! Even at home, most of the time, she's sweet, kind, and funny. Our firm boundaries lead to her yelling, "I don't care; I'm going to kick you in the face; I'm mean and stupid, and you think so, too." A few times, we've had to physically restrain her to keep her from hurting us, herself, or her two-year-old brother.

With time to cool off, she is back to herself. Both the negative self-

talk and the physical violence worry me. Is it starting kindergarten?
Is something(s) in her environment the trigger (I've been commuting
long hours this year)? Or is there is something really off that needs
professional attention?

You're right to worry about how intensely your daughter reacts
to frustration, fatigue, and hunger. I'm sure it's worst when all three
are combined. Family stress, your frequent absences, and starting
kindergarten are likely all part of why she reaches the boiling point
so often, despite her basic sweet temperament. Often the best way
to "diagnose" whether a problem is environmental/situational or
developmental/personality-driven is to alter the situation and see if
the problem resolves. The fact that she behaves well at school tells
you that she has the capacity to hold herself together for a pretty
long time. The "meltdowns" result from either end-of-the-day fatigue
or coming/being home (or all of those). Keeping herself together at
school may be such a strain that she falls apart at home. If so, I'd
expect the tantrums very soon after you pick her up or get home.
Many parents are baffled by the "angel at school; demon at home"
syndrome. Rest assured:

1. It's common
2. It's better this way than the other way around.

Here's how I'd start:

1. Institute "special time" when you pick her up and before you
    drive home. This should include: a healthy snack, a short
    walk, reviewing her day, or progressive relaxation (See #4)
    in the car parked in your driveway (before going inside). You
    do it too; you'll be amazed!
2. Often the trouble is transitioning from structured activities
    at school to unstructured time at home. While driving, plan
    exactly what she'll do once she's home.
3. Chart when outbursts occur. Is it mostly in the late
    afternoon? Does she need rest? A snack? Is it when you and

your husband must divide your attention between her, her brother, each other, and preparing dinner? Make a "pre-emptive action plan" with a set sequence of snack, rest, and activities.

4. Use relaxation techniques. Kids can easily go on "a trip" of imagined soothing landscapes, or learn "progressive relaxation." With eyes closed, start from the toes and go up the body all the way to fingers and face, tightening the muscles to the count of one, two, three, and then releasing.

5. Plan more time alone with you, with no person, no phones, and no tasks competing for your attention. Pick three weekly "special times." No big undertakings! A twenty-minute stroll, doing a puzzle together, playing dress-up, or reading a favorite book are good activities to fill these moments.

6. Have a heart-to-heart talk when she is cheerful. Say you can see how angry she gets and how upsetting it is for everyone. Tell her the mean things she says about herself and you are not true. Then drop it; the more you react to these statements, the more she'll know they yank your chain.

7. Make a book together: each page for something that makes her angry. She can draw the thing itself or how she feels about it. The more pages you can fill together, the more "containers" you are providing her for her anger.

8. Set up an "I'm really mad spot" with a punching bag, newspapers to tear, paper and crayons. Encourage and praise her for using it when she's angry.

9. Read *Alexander and the Horrible, Terrible, No-good, Very Bad Day*. Over and over.

10. Make it clear verbally, and by physically restraining her if needed, that you won't let her hurt anyone; neither you, nor your husband, nor her brother, nor other kids, nor herself.

If three to four weeks go by with no improvement, definitely seek professional help.

Sibling Rivalry: School-Age

Our two kids used to get along well. My eight-year-old daughter was fairly tolerant of her rambunctious, sometimes annoying (it's the truth!) six-year-old brother who always wants to tag along with her. But recently, she pushes him away (mostly verbally, sometimes with a little physical gesture to make her point) when she's busy with an activity or—even more so—when she has a friend over. When he begs her or bugs her, she comes to me or my wife and demands we "get him off her back." At the same time, I've also noticed since he started first grade this year that he measures himself against her and, of course, can't make the grade. He will break down in bitter tears when he struggles over homework and she looks at his worksheet and says, "It's easy! Six plus four is ten!" He is utterly crestfallen when he can't keep up with her. How can I manage things so that they get along better and don't compete so much?

It sounds like you are in one of those sibling rivalry vortices that will come and go in your children's lives as their relationship develops. Hopefully, these periods will wane as they mature, and their relationship as adults will be close and sustaining.

Sibling rivalry and competition is a good thing, up to a point, so let me start by enumerating its benefits (then we'll talk about keeping it in moderation and helping each of your kids negotiate it).

1. Sibling relations are, hopefully, lifelong and foundational to a person's sense of themselves and their love and commitment to their family.

2. Sibling rivalry mostly manifests at home, where you, the parent, are present and available to help negotiate, address hurt feelings, model and encourage being considerate, and demand apologies when they are called for. Out in the world, your children deal with similar challenges without your benign presence and guidance, so what you do at home provides them with essential tools for handling their relationships with friends and classmates.

3. Sometimes rivalry arises when there are big developmental differences between your kids; when one has taken a leap and the other is still their old self. Understanding that maturing and mastering skills and knowledge take a long time and a lot of effort is a good lesson for each child. The older girl learns to be proud of her achievements but also compassionate toward her younger brother, who's got a lot of catching up to do. The younger boy learns about patience and perseverance: he *will* one day, soon or not so soon, be able to do all the things his sister can do.

4. At least some of the time, you have an opportunity to turn the rivalry into compassion and/or collaboration. Next time your daughter says, "It's easy," ask her if she'll show her brother her "tricks" for making it so easy. Or, when she has a friend over and the little guy tries to butt in, tell him, "Let them play on their own. This means *you* have *me* all to yourself."

That said, I have not forgotten the moments when sibling rivalry is painful and you get dragged into impossible-to-mediate situations. So here are some guidelines for handling those moments:

1. Start by observing: Is this a situation where you think your kids could sort things out by themselves? You can encourage that by saying, "I have to take care of something right now, can you two can work it out on your own?" You may need to make a small suggestion to get them started.

2. Have a conversation with your daughter about the situation, away from her brother's ears. Help her come up with two or three simple activities she would allow her brother to join her in, e.g., arranging her stuffed animals in a row on her bed by size, building something together with Legos. He would even be thrilled to help her clean up her room! In exchange, make a list of activities she reasonably wants to exclude him from (hopefully, it's not too long).

3. Have a parallel conversation and drawing up of lists with

your son. Have him write or dictate activities he'd like his sister to join him in/help him with and a second one of things he wants her out of.

4. Post the lists on the bulletin board and facilitate a conversation with the two of them going over them and agreeing to respect each other's wishes.

5. Make a plan with your son of special activities he can do (some with you, others on his own) when his sister has a friend over. Make these activities special by, for example, pulling out a game or a puzzle set aside just for this occasion. And, of course, have his friend or friends come over for a playdate, if feasible, at the same time.

6. Post the lists in each of their rooms and add stickers (or points toward a reward) for each time they do a shared activity in peace. For your son, also dispense stickers when he lets his sister do her thing without butting in.

7. When a small miracle happens and a day passes in harmony and cooperation, make it known that you noticed and appreciated it. Three good days in a row merit a special outing or activity they both enjoy.

Don't aim for eternal peace! You'll be disappointed. Conflicts will bubble up. When they do, try to help your kids sort them out by talking instead of screaming, crying, or hitting. You will likely need to act as a facilitator. Try for that, rather than being a referee: better for *them* come up with a solution, though some days that will be only a wish.

Further reading: Adele Faber and Elaine Mazlish, *Sibling without Rivalry* and *Peaceful Parent, Happy Siblings*.

Yelling at My Kids: Help Me Stop!

I have two wonderful kids whom I love more than anything. I am married, work outside the house, and am generally the main caretaker.

My boys (ten and eight) are usually great kids. We have occasional issues with them arguing and fighting, which turns into them yelling, which turns into me yelling, and the hamster wheel starts. I know their behavior is learned from my example. And honestly, I have opened my eyes and realized my example is no example! Lately, I seem to find myself yelling out of frustration more than ever. Then I feel so guilty and hate myself for it. I feel like such a failure as a parent when this happens.

I am willing to be open and work on things that I need to change. I just do not have any idea where to start!

Yelling is such a common pitfall of parenthood. I commend you for your honesty, first and foremost with yourself! I suggest beginning with reflecting on what may be underlying causes. Let me suggest a few common ones:

1. Reproducing, despite your vows to the contrary, family-of-origin patterns: your mother or father yelling at you, yelling between parents, or yelling between siblings.

2. The transition from physically controlling your child in infancy to early toddlerhood to "remote voice control." It's so much easier! But often, "voice control" imperceptibly grows from clear, firm directions to ever-louder orders as your child tests your limits. At first, raising your voice seems very effective, but before you know it, you are yelling way too often. Some parents (I gather that, thankfully, you are not one of them) "graduate" to spanking.

3. "Drained batteries:" You are too exhausted, overwhelmed, or stressed by other things in your life. Your self-control goes out the window. Yelling replaces thoughtful reasoning, negotiation, and firm limit setting.

Begin by trying to pinpoint what underlies the yelling; try to determine what triggers it. If you have a partner who's around when you yell, ask them to be a quiet observer for a few days and accept their assessment (no defensiveness!) of when/where/what triggers yelling. But I bet you are alone with the kids when you yell. So, if you can, run a video camera (or your iPhone) for several days during "the yelling hours." It won't take long before you forget about the recording and revert to your habitual behavior. Then watch and learn. By the way, listening to/watching yourself yell may be the easiest "homemade aversion therapy" (pairing unpleasant sensations with behavior you want to eliminate). How? Listen or watch a half dozen times: soon, you'll find yourself holding back the hollering as this "tape" turns on the instant before.

Once you've identified likely times and triggers, reorganize your routine to eliminate or bypass these. For example, if your kids get home from school hungry and demanding, and that's when you're likely to blow, have a snack in the car before you even get home. Or put snacks out before you leave in the morning, ready for afternoon arrivals. Add a structured quiet activity right after snack, such as working on a 500-piece puzzle. Alternatively, your kids might need the opposite: four or more laps around the school track before going home.

Or create a "DIY aversion therapy" by wearing a rubber band on your wrist, snapping it pretty hard each time you yell. Belt out an "ouch!" when you snap it: it'll ingrain the message faster. Pair this with rewarding yourself each time you step back from the "yelling brink." Don't be embarrassed to be a bit childish about it: a point on the tally page, a penny in a jar, or a sticker on a chart for each success. Cash these in for dollars toward a "guilty pleasure:" hours of time off on the weekend (your partner picking up the slack), time in a spa, dinner out with a friend. You get the idea: make it concrete, reward each "un-yelling," setting your heart on something fabulous.

If none of these steps work, I recommend working with a family therapist. Yelling rarely disappears by itself. You want to get it out of your family's repertoire before your kids hit puberty.

Teaching Kids to Succeed at Failure

I overheard at the locker room: "We don't put our daughter

in any situation in which she is not certain to succeed." *Oh, my,* I thought to myself, *what a deprived child!* You probably agree... but, be honest with yourself, how often have you tried to set things up for your child so they are guaranteed a success? Very often, I would guess. Of course! As parents, we want to pave our children's path in golden bricks. But, as a rule, parents these days have gone way overboard, as the oft-cited terms "helicopter parents" and "snowplow parents" demonstrate.

Why not? you might ask. *Shouldn't I shield my young child from the heartbreak of losing a game, the disappointment of not getting picked for a team, the frustration of not scoring the winning goal?* Simply put: because handling the emotional impact of failure and forging ahead after it are crucial life skills.

Begin by reflecting on yourself and your spouse or parenting partner: what are your strategies? Can you admit to yourself when you've failed, acknowledge the emotional sting without too much self-recrimination (let alone blaming others for it) and find a way forward? How would you translate your strategies to smaller, simpler steps for your young child? Can you put them into little "lessons" or anecdotes you feel comfortable sharing with your child?

Now you're ready for some tips:

1. Kids under age four don't yet have much in their emotional tool kit. It is fine to try to structure their lives so that disappointments and failures happen within your protective orbit. For example, you might purposefully work on a puzzle with them that's a bit too hard and say something like, "This puzzle is really hard. Will you let mommy help you with this piece?" Then celebrate succeeding together. Similarly, when the child is throwing a ball: you can start with a target (basketball, net) too far and then explicate, "We put the goal too far. Would you like to move it closer in?" Here you are problem-solving together.

2. Starting at age four, you can encourage your child to take more

risks and try more things she may not be able to accomplish yet. A bit of forewarning may temper the reaction, e.g., "Try to hit the nail right on the head to get it to go in. It's hard... so let's see if you can do it by yourself. If not, I can help you, just a little bit." Now stand back and watch as your child attempts it on her own. Encourage expressing frustration in words, rather than physically, and figuring out a way to get it done (maybe together) if the first effort fails.

3. Tell stories about your own failures: they can be childhood anecdotes or adult experiences. The lesson should emphasize patience, persevering, and eventual success, but don't make it too glowing. You don't want your child to feel that you always get it right in the end while he can't.

4. Remember that you're trying to equip your child with language for their feelings and tools for self-soothing and self-reassurance. With kids ages four to six, it's best to stick to a succinct vocabulary with drawings, emojis, or facial expression stickers for feelings such as "disappointed, sad, frustrated, angry, discouraged." Keep an ear out for the natural tendency to blame others or outside circumstances (e.g., "the ball was deflated" or "the finish line was crooked") and gently guide your child into taking responsibility for his actions and limitations. Your support is crucial: mostly plenty of hugs and high-fives. Medals, certificates of achievement, and ribbons are good additions: first for effort and perseverance and, later, for accomplishment.

5. For kids age six and up, I suggest having your child create a treasure box of self-encouragement. It can include statements written in advance and placed in the box (some clichés, such as "If you fail, try, try again," are fine), photos of herself at moments of success in new tasks, gold stars, and even little treats — some kind of "super-power chocolates."

6. Help your child narrate the process of trying and failing, how

it feels in the moment, and self-talk about not giving up, trying a different way, and so on. This can be told (or dictated if your child is not a proficient writer yet) as a story, writing in a journal, drawing a cartoon, etc. Despite the preponderance of electronic writing and image-making, I strongly recommend creating a physical object: it has much greater power as a container for your child's experience and feelings.

7. Encourage your child to revisit these records of failure and frustration a few days after they occur, then after a couple of weeks and, finally, some months later. It will give him a concrete sense of how the passage of time and his maturation help him get better at "succeeding at failure."

In Praise of Child Labor

I know: what a strange title! But bear with me. You see, I grew up on a kibbutz in Israel and, like anyone in this country who was raised on a farm, started working early in life. Starting in kindergarten, we kids worked in our own small vegetable garden as well as cleaning up after ourselves alongside our caretakers, be it our showers, playrooms, or dining tables. In third grade, I got assigned a rotation working with the dairy cows. What an honor! It was the most coveted position: doing the" real work" of adults. You had to prove yourself first in the children's farm, where we had sheep, goats, chickens, and peacocks along with a vegetable garden, but no cows. Cows were the big time!

On my first day on the job, I got brief instructions on how to lead the cows from the grazing pasture back to the dairy for the evening milking. Imagine me at the time: not yet four feet tall, skinny (alas, those days are over) and scab-kneed, leading 120 Holsteins home. There were gates to open and close guiding the cows, and I had a stick to goad them, but I do wonder how the adults in charge came to believe I could manage this on my own (not to mention what the cows made of me).

It was a formative moment, as you can tell from the fact that I still want to write (and crow) about it over fifty years later. The stint with the cows led to many other jobs around the kibbutz, the level of responsibility growing as we matured. For our bar and bat mitzvahs (the whole class celebrated together, and each child complete twelve individual tasks), all of us had to work a full, eight-hour day in a branch of the kibbutz. I got unlucky here: assigned to work in the communal dining room. I would have preferred the sugar beet fields or the date palm groves. But, like the adult members, I went where the kibbutz's daily work assignments needed me. I cleaned all forty or fifty windows on each side so that they shone at the end of the day. And so did I!

So, what does all of that have to do with parenting in 2020? This is my unabashed recommendation: make your children work! From an early age (four or five), your kids should learn about the responsibility, physical effort, modest boredom, and great sense of achievement that comes with manual labor. I know you don't have a dairy farm on hand, but you do have garbage to clear and recycling to sort, a house to clean (even if you have a house cleaner, get your child involved in cleaning after themselves), garden or patio plants to tend, rugs to vacuum (kids *love* vacuuming: such power!), floors to sweep, dishes to wash.

In truth, most work today—likely what you do yourself—involves minimal physical exertion, so our kids are deprived (I mean it: they are missing out!) of the pleasures of manual labor. Try to create opportunities for it in your home. Or find an urban farm where you can volunteer, a community garden to join, a park or beach to clean up, or an elderly neighbor who can use help in the yard. Check with your child's school or afterschool program: do they provide opportunities for manual skills like carpentry or leatherwork? Can they integrate the children into the cleanup work needed in the school? Can the students plant a garden?

Once your child really understands the concept of money, working for pay is a valuable experience as well. But honestly, it does not compare to the gains of work for its own rewards or to help someone in need. Try it. You might find that your child's enthusiasm for work spills over to you.

Allowance for Young Children

My first grader has informed me that our family is woefully behind the times in the financial arena. "Everybody," he said," has an allowance! I am the only one in class who is poor!"

I wasn't sure what to say, so I told him we'd think about it. I called some class parents and got the full bell curve between "no way" to "he's had an allowance since he was four." What do you think in general? What's a reasonable amount? Should there be strings attached, such as doing his chores, cooperating at home, or finishing his homework and getting good grades?

This is one of these questions that has a different answer for each family. It depends on how *you* relate to money, your financial situation, and your attitude toward consumption. While we've all acquiesced to the idea that "Money makes the world go 'round," we need not agree to it running our family life. If it's important to you to have a family atmosphere where money is not held as a value, you might want to take a stand "against the grain" here. You could say: "For our family, money is no more than what you use to buy what we need. We don't want it to influence our relationships. Instead of an allowance, let's talk about the things you need and want, and together we'll make good decisions about what to buy."

Another view is that handling money is an important life skill and parents ought to teach their kids how to manage it from early on. An allowance provides an opportunity to instill key concepts: earning your rewards, saving, planning how to use your assets, and giving to charity. If this is your inclination, consider these suggestions:

1. Do some field research so that the amount of your weekly allowance is comfortably in the middle range among your

son's friends. Or use this rule of thumb: a dollar for each year of age (eight years old =$8/week) when only about half is spent each week, and the rest is put aside for savings and tzedakah [charity] (more on that below).

2. A weekly allowance is perfect for elementary school kids. Middle school kids can "graduate" to a monthly allowance with the greater freedom and responsibility of planning for larger sums.

3. Have a "financial planning meeting" with your son in which you go over what kinds of things he'll spend his allowance on and devise "Savings" and "Tzedakah" plans. For the latter two I recommend you institute some kind of match: for every dollar your son puts into a tzedakah box, you put one in as well. For kids under age nine you want an actual transparent box/jar so they can see the coins and bills pile up.

4. For the "savings plan," you might match at fifty cents to the dollar. The savings can be split into sums: one set aside toward a purchase within the short term (two to three weeks for ages six to seven; an additional week for every year of age thereafter) and, longer-term, three months and up. Starting at nine or ten, you can open an actual savings account at the bank.

5. The allowance should be contingent on your child's satisfying their basic family obligations each week, from cooperating in getting ready for school and cleaning up toys, to household chores (three to five per week).

6. You can let your child earn extra money with jobs around the house and for neighbors. But be sure to balance earning money for work with teaching your child (primarily through modeling) about acts of kindness done voluntarily, for no material gain.

7. Some parents wonder about paying their children for good grades. While I recognize that this may have significant

merit for high-risk kids in families and environments with minimal support for excelling in school, I do not favor it as a general rule. Schoolwork should be seen as a fundamental obligation, and success should be its own reward (more on school and motivation in a future chapter).

Finally, watch how you and your spouse talk about money: are you manifesting your values, or are you being sucked in by our culture's infatuation with wealth?

Lying (and Stealing)

My five-year-old nephew, unusually bright (really! you should hear the things he says) came home from school one day with his pockets bulging suspiciously. When his mother asked what was in his pockets, he said, "Nothing." She gave him a moment to think about it and then asked to look. Calmly, she asked if he took the Lego pieces from school. He said "no." She said she could tell they were from school and that he'd made a "bad decision" taking them and lying about it. He made a beeline for his room. Minutes later, she knocked and entered, finding him scrunched under his bed. She coaxed him out with, "I'm not angry, but it's important that you tell me the truth. Even if you did something wrong." The boy cried and emptied his pockets. He was too upset to explain why he did it, but it was obvious to his mom, who knew what a Lego-lover he is.

Mom gave a short spiel about stealing, and why it's wrong and told the boy he would have to return the Legos to the teacher the next day and apologize. He blanched and pleaded: "How about if I just bring them back and put them in the bin when nobody's looking?" Mom said "No," he had to own up for what he had done. The shame was part of the lesson. He ran to his room and slid under the bed again. She let him be. A while later, he came out of his room with a smile on his face. "How about if I send the pieces to school in the mail?" As I said, he's very bright.

Both Mom and Dad thought this was pretty ingenious, but decided it was still avoidance and told him he must return the pieces and face the teacher. He didn't eat much dinner and went to sleep in tears. The next morning, Dad took him to school and stood right by his side as he returned the Legos and told the teacher he was sorry. She said she was happy to see that after he did something wrong, he understood it was so, brought the Legos back, and said he was sorry. "That was brave," the teacher said and patted his head, even as he couldn't look her in the eye.

Lying is, as most parents have seen, an integral part of growing up. It starts innocently enough when your child does not yet have a firm grasp on the difference between reality and wishful fantasy. Soon, he learns what a useful tool it is (until caught) for wiggling out of tight spots ("I didn't touch the iPhone") and getting what he wants: ("No, Mommy didn't give me the cookie she promised for after dinner").

Around age five is the optimal time to start tracking lies more carefully and confronting your child when they resort to them because, by that age, most kids have a firm grasp on what's true and what's not. Did the parents do the right thing? Certainly, confronting his actions, explaining the importance of telling the truth, making things right, and apologizing, and standing by him, are all key. I do wonder if the parents might have met the boy halfway and supported his "creative problem-solving." That would have demonstrated to him the benefit of telling the truth. Of course, this would depend on the specific personality of the child. For this boy, I trust the parents knew he could handle the embarrassment and learn his lesson.

For a different child, a possible alternative scenario would be saying something like "If you took the Lego pieces without permission, that is stealing. If you tell me the truth, I'll help you find a way to return them that will not be too embarrassing [perhaps, indeed, mailing the Legos with a written note]. If you lie and I find out from the teacher, you'll have to return the Legos to the teacher and apologize to her face-to-face."

Step one of teaching kids not to lie is helping them articulate why they lied and getting to the greed, anger, envy, hurt, or other difficult emotions that lead to it. Once you empathize with the feeling behind the lying, talk with your child about other ways he could have addressed the situation.

II. School Issues

Competition with Classmates

My second-grader has loved school since the day she entered her kindergarten class. School has been a magical place for her until the middle of second grade, when math quizzes were introduced and she discovered that she is not "the best math wiz" (her words). Other kids have been faster than her. When I tell her that it's not about speed, she says, "Yes, but they also always get the answers right... and I don't." She has become almost obsessed with measuring herself against other kids, especially two girls whom she favors as playmates.

I want to help her be less competitive, but I also know competition is how much of the world actually does work, and I want her to be prepared. What should I do?

This day was bound to come sooner or later. Some schools put a lot of thought and effort into creating a noncompetitive atmosphere and, if you are lucky, your child is in such a school. But most schools rely on testing and grades, which are so much easier to administer than an individualized way of fostering and assessing children's learning.

I would start with a conversation about competition in which you emphasize that some things in life are very competitive with success and results easy to measure. Other, often more important things (to you, at least, I hope) are not. What I mean is two columns, one for competitive activities with clear, measurable parameters of success, such as solving math problems fast, sprinting, and jumping. The second column is for noncompetitive, generally unquantifiable activities, such as enjoying your work and play, kindness, and cooperation. Spend plenty of time on developing the list and have your child circle the activities on it that are most important to her. If she asks your opinion, give it gently, with an emphasis on column number two.

Next, help your child with an honest assessment of herself: what is she best at? What does she enjoy the most? Hopefully, on her list will be things like helping her friends, enjoying herself, and being creative. Hone in on the things she says she's not that good at. First of all—is her assessment realistic? If not, a joint parent-teacher-child conference is in order.

If she is realistic and has some areas where she falls short of her expectations (or yours or the teacher's), it's time to develop an action plan. Consider all or some of these:

1. Extra time for the task (at home and/or in class)
2. Tutoring (by you or a professional)
3. Meeting with the teacher to adjust expectations
4. In cases of significant issues, your child is *entitled* to an evaluation by the school psychologist or learning specialist and an individualized educational plan.

That done, it's time to work together to create a clear goal, work plan, and time table for how she'll improve, and to her help with ideas and encouragement. Usually, just meeting her own expectations will be rewarding enough in itself. There should be no need for prizes. However, recognition from her teacher and additional family members is certainly in order.

Sometimes, competitive feelings are more about social status than academic performance. How do you ferret that out? If the name of one child (especially another girl in the case of our daughter or a boy if you have one) keeps coming up as the "rival," it's probably that. Open up a conversation about friendship and who's whose friend in class. Creating a visual map with different colored lines between kids indicating levels of friendships can help a lot in visualizing the situation.

If the rival in question seems to be the queen bee, talk with your child about her feelings, which may be very mixed. She may want this girl's friendship more than anything, so envy of other girls, anger, frustration, and negative feelings about herself may all be part of the cauldron of emotions. You need to assess (perhaps with the aid of her teacher) what is best for your daughter. Hopefully, it's fostering a healthy friendship, but sometimes the best approach is avoiding the "queen" and finding other friends. Help with suggestions of steps to take in the chosen direction.

Finally, it's constructive simply to name the feeling of competitiveness and to share simplified anecdotes about when you and other adults have felt and acted competitive, with the consequences—sometimes positive, sometimes not.

Too Much Homework

The school year is less than a month in, and already my daughter is drowning in homework. We're embroiled in almost daily struggles over it. She is in third grade. On good days, when she is cooperative, focused, and has had a healthy snack, and the homework includes a lot of math (which she loves and rips through), it takes her about an hour to finish. On bad days, it can be over ninety minutes. There's no time left for anything else, and, needless to say, we're either helping her or goading her to keep working. I've talked to friends whose kids are in other schools (both public and private), and it's pretty much the same story.

It's ruining our family time, and I doubt re she's absorbing much beyond frustration and a growing hatred of homework. What do you suggest?

You don't quite come out and say it, but I read between the lines and agree wholeheartedly: that's an egregious amount of homework. To be honest, I am not a fan of homework in elementary school at all. I am sure some teachers will jump at me, but I don't believe it adds much to real learning, and it does quite a bit of damage. It's robbing young children of the free, unstructured playtime they still need, strains parent-child relations, and sours kids on learning by diminishing the joys of self-driven discovery and mastery. Frankly, it makes no sense to me that kids are in school for six to seven hours, nearly a full workday, and they can't finish the day's tasks. Of course, so many of us have the same struggle at work—taking work home nearly every day—but it's not a good thing! Not for adults and certainly not for children.

In reality, I know a lot of teachers agree with me but feel pressured to assign homework to meet parents' expectations, not the children's needs. There is also a notion that you should prepare kids for the harder schedules and pressures of middle and high school by starting them early in the overworked track. I think it would be better to do the exact opposite.

Now, that was probably not helpful in navigating the actual situation you are in, as I doubt showing this chapter to the teachers would convince them to cancel homework. Nevertheless, I would start with a meeting with the teacher, focusing on the *goals* of the homework. Once the teacher provides a clear and sensible set of goals (beyond just drilling class material), you can look at those and together work out a strategy to accomplish them (or at least come close) without ninety minutes of torture.

I suspect that a fifteen-minute review of the core lessons covered each day would be much more effective in reinforcing the lessons than much longer drilling. Could the teacher email/post those on a school website/blog? You can also discuss with the teacher more creative ways to reinforce the lessons such as making up treasure hunts, mysteries, or putting on skits.

Second, work with your daughter on setting up a regular homework schedule and let her know she needs to show you she is working attentively for fifteen minutes, regardless of how much she finishes. Give her a thirty-minutes break that includes a snack, open-ended conversation about her day (especially fun things), and free play, but no screen time. Next, have another fifteen minutes of homework under the same terms. That's enough.

Ask her to estimate how much she can do of each assignment before she starts. It's a useful skill and a win-win situation. If she overestimates what she can finish, compliment her ambition and hard work, despite her not meeting her own expectations. If she does more than she had estimated she could, praise her for that and add a small "bonus," such as extra time for a favorite activity or a sticker or point toward a small prize. If she seems to purposefully underestimate what she can complete, guaranteeing she earns the bonus, let a few days go by and nudge her to raise her expectations.

Help! My Son Is a Bully

I am heartbroken and embarrassed to write this, but I must face the truth: my son is a bully. It started inconspicuously in third grade when he teased some of the younger, less athletic kids in his class. But now that he is in fifth grade, I see that he's turned into a bully. I want to blame the two other boys in his "little gang," but that's a copout.

He used to be pleasant and cooperative at home (he's an only child, so no sibling relationship issues), but recently, I have noticed some of that behavior leaching into our family life. He's ornery, speaks to us in a dismissive tone, and rolls his eyes when we reprimand him or make requests and demands. My husband says I'm overreacting, but

I think he's in denial. He has a "man's man" exterior himself and says our son is just a typical boy. I don't even know where to start. Help!

You are wise (and brave!) to see your son's behavior as bullying. While there's plenty of advice and support for parents and kids being bullied, there's not nearly enough for the bullies. You are absolutely right to be concerned. If it turns out your worries are justified, intervening early is crucial.

Begin with a systematic investigation: turn to the school to inquire if your son's teachers and schoolyard attendants have noticed any bullying. If your son hangs out with two other bullies, he may be clever enough to hide his tracks, so inquire about the behavior of the other boys (letting the school know you understand maintaining confidentiality). You might consider hiring a child therapist or other appropriate professional (e.g., a shadow teacher already at the school assisting special-needs kids) to observe your son a few times.

If you discover that, indeed, your son is bullying kids at school, you need to address it directly with him, in a way that is both firm and supportive. If you don't trust yourself and your husband to pull this off, get help: from a therapist, a youth counselor, your rabbi or minister, or a trusted friend who's "good with kids."

Make it clear to your son that:

1. Bullying is unacceptable and often escalates with time and will land him in bigger and bigger trouble.

2. You understand that this is coming from serious distress inside him and that you will be supportive and help him with whatever it may be. You should consider the following possibilities (among others, based on what you know about your son). Is he:

    •   Feeling isolated, lonely, unable to make the kind of friends he really wants? This is often the underlying cause of bullying.

    •   Struggling with depression?

- Insecure about his academic abilities and performance?
- Anxious about athletic achievement or other activities that are too competitive for him?
- Worried about his sexual/gender identity?
- Showing other signs of distress, such as lying, stealing?

Let him know that there are programs to help him overcome bullying. These can take a variety of forms: child individual therapy or group therapy, joining an anti-bullying campaign/organization for kids. There are many options. Find a locally-based one, such as Beyond Differences (www.beyonddifferences.org), which trains teens in California to champion school communities where no one is marginalized, and its partner, No Bully (http://www.nobully.org), which provides in-school interventions. Pacer's National Bullying Prevention Center has a simple (simple-minded but a place to start) "Am I a Bully" checklist (www.pacerkidsagainstbullying.org/kab/do-you-bully/).

Ask yourself: are there subtle behaviors at home (or his sports team?) that may give the impression that bullying is cool? It can be as innocuous as kidding around in a mock-bullying way or more obvious, like violent TV programs and video games.

What you hope will follow these conversations (be patient: it'll take time, overcoming false starts, some denial, and anger) is sufficient insight into why your son is bullying. Next, you want to help him understand the impact of his behavior and develop empathy for his victims. After arriving at this point, he needs to make new friends—in and out of school.

Finally comes active engagement in an alternative: joining an anti-bullying campaign at his school or with another local group.

"Going Green" Gone Too Far?

My seven-year-old twin girls came home from school announcing they can't go to their grandparents for Passover: They have renounced (not their word) flying. They actually used the term "carbon footprint" about airplane pollution! They also won't eat any food that comes in a plastic or saran-wrap package, and I can't throw anything in the garbage without their approval. They are so proud of what they've learned in school! I am all for saving the planet, but this is going too far! How do I support their enthusiasm but place reasonable limits on their "green dictatorship?"

You have very bright kids on your hands, so that'll help. But, as I am sure you already know, seven-year-olds think they are smarter than anyone and can be bossy... So, let's separate the good intentions and important environmental lessons from kids lording it over their parents.

Start with a conversation: *What did you learn at school about "going green?"* Listen for subtle underlying anxiety about what "global warming" means. Some kids this age do grasp the overall issue but leap to thinking that their everyday safety is threatened. Your kids' "Extreme Green-over" may reflect such fears.

After sorting out the big picture, make a list together: one column for changes in your family's lifestyle that are reasonable, the other for those that are not, such as abandoning your car or never flying again. Treat the draconian options with humor, adding some absurdities like "No more going to the moon for lunch." It will be fun and will soften your daughters' militancy. Introduce the idea that many decisions in life involve weighing competing values; rarely is anything is 100 percent good or bad. How? Play a game I call "You Be the Judge." Pose ethical dilemmas as questions where the answer is ambiguous and let them struggle for their own solutions. My son loved this game at exactly this age. He is now a practicing lawyer, having graduated from NYU Law School (as the class valedictorian): who knows if the game played a role in that?

Explain that Passover with the family trumps the carbon footprint of flying, but suggest balancing it by planting trees: in your yard, at your kid's school, or contact the Parks and Recreation Department to organize a group of neighbors to plant at a nearby park. See if there is an educational farm in your community where you can participate in planting, harvesting, and other farming activities.

Harness the enthusiasm at home:

1. Put your kids in charge of the recycling, including sorting and taking it to the curb.

2. Have them make charts of the weekly weight of recycling versus garbage, aiming for more and less, respectively.

3. If your community provides food scraps/garden vegetation collection, put your kids in charge of that too. If not, get them involved in contacting City Hall or starting a petition for it in your town.

4. Plant a garden at home, however small. If you are in an apartment, set boxes in the windows. Start with radishes! They sprout in four days and mature in thirty to forty: a perfect time frame for the patience of seven-year-olds. Radishes may not be their favorite veggie, but try my childhood recipe: bread spread thick with honey and dotted with thinly-sliced radishes.

5. Go to the farmers' market together and let each child pick two items.

6. If you are Jewish (even if not), learn the traditional blessings *(brachot)* for fruits and vegetables together and add these to your dinner routine. Try to pause and appreciate the marvel of food coming from the earth.

7. Record everything in a "Green Album:" recycling vs. garbage weight charts, planting records, photos, and so on. Help your kids make an electronic version they can share with friends or make into a class project.

Whatever you end up doing (I assume only some of the things suggested), have your kids in charge as much as possible. All these tasks provide great opportunities for collaboration among family members, an additional benefit. They'll grow not only their radishes and environmental responsibility, but also independence, reasoning skills, helpfulness at home, and cooperation.

End-of-Summer Blues

The end of August is near, and we need your advice to plan activities for our two boys, ages eight and five. Both have had a full summer of sports, arts, and science camps. In past years we've gone camping as a family. The first three days were an endless string of complaints (No TV? No video games? No sleeping in?). By the time they finally adjusted, we had only two days left. The week before school was a mad scramble to get ready.

This year, we can't take off that much time, and school starts earlier. We are looking at two weeks with NO PROGRAM. Part of me feels like the kids deserve downtime and just "vegging out," but another part worries they'll drive each other (and us) crazy or spend all their time glued to screens. What's a reasonable balance? How do we make the last two weeks of August a treat rather than a torture?

The challenge of the end of summer is on many parents' minds when it looms. While for parents who need to work full schedules, it's childcare and supervision, you and many others puzzle over how much "vegging out" and screen time to allow and how to entertain bored, antsy kids.

I am of the school that believes most kids are overscheduled, overstressed, overstimulated by screens, and in overly competitive environments. During the school year, they are wrung dry by demanding schoolwork, too much homework, sports, music lessons, art activities, and time-pressured family routines. Two weeks of "downtime" can be a great blessing and, if you manage it right, open up time for free play and creativity that get shut out by most kids' excessive dose of results-oriented activities.

I would suggest that no structured activities and minimal screen time (none would be best if you can handle it), sure to lead to boredom, would be a great gift. It will create an opportunity for your boys to generate their own ideas for engagement, as well as learning to be alone with their feelings and thoughts. These experiences are disappearing from our kids' (and our own) lives. I hate to sound like a Luddite, but I believe that total immersion in information and constant communication are impoverishing kids' inner lives and dismantling the magic of play.

But enough of my preaching. I suggest you set the general parameters and let your children exercise maximum autonomy managing their time, using this practical guide for the two weeks:

1. Declare the first week "vegging-out time" and let them do as close to nothing as possible. Don't suggest or provide activities or entertainment but encourage (and assist if needed) anything they come up with relying only on their own resources.

2. Take the total amount of daily screen time you allow during the school year and triple it (assuming it's roughly one hour a day during school time), multiply by the number of days ahead of you. That's the number of hours in their "Screen-Time Bank." If they want to use their time to binge on TV and video games for the first days, let them. With a younger child, use paper "tickets" to represent each hour of screen time so he can "see his time."

3. If you are very active and accomplishment-oriented, it may be hard to tolerate your kids sitting around doing nothing. Try this graduated schedule with a good dose of humor:

On Day One, your kids need not lift a finger; on Day Two, they should do only what requires two fingers; Day Three: one hand; Day Four: two hands; Day Five: hands and one foot. You get the idea. I bet you anything that by Day Four, your kids will beg you to let them do more, even unload the dishwasher.

Finally, if you can manage to have two days of downtime yourself during this period, it will be a great boon to you and the whole family. Much more worthwhile, I would argue, than finally cleaning the garage or organizing your closets.

PART IV: Family Relations and Difficult Times

I. Grave Illness, Death, and Challenging Times in the Family

Mothering with Breast Cancer: Against Invulnerability

*E*rin Hyman wrote the following column while battling breast cancer *as a young mother. I could not begin to imagine, let alone dare to write about the valley of shadows she was traversing. She writes about how she can look her children in the eye and be reassuring without disguising the truth, supportive with neither false promises nor make-believe invulnerability.*

"I came prepared to cry," a mother in our support group (BAYS: Bay Area Young Survivors) said as we began our meeting, "because I haven't let myself do that at home, not wanting my kids to see it." Another friend told me she didn't let her children see her even once without a wig. As mothers of young children, in various phases of treatment, we must, of course, put our children's welfare first. It's not only the first consideration when debating treatment options and the primary worry in regards to being incapacitated, even temporarily. It also dictates how we let ourselves process the raw emotions we experience.

Afraid and overwhelmed, mothers want more than anything to shield their children from anxiety and the brute force of their emotions. But I disagree. Trying to shield our children entirely from what we're going through comes at a great cost—to both them and us. I don't think it does any of us a service to maintain a veneer of invulnerability.

From the beginning, my husband and I spoke to our children frankly and directly about my cancer and what they could expect to happen. My eldest, eight and relentlessly inquisitive, asked questions constantly: "How did you get this? How long will you be in the hospital? Are there any other side effects of chemo that you haven't told me about?" My younger son, a kindergartener, had an understanding more limited to the practical: "Who will pick me up from school?"

Their initial anxieties focused on "the hair thing." They really didn't want me to lose mine and *really* didn't want anyone to see me bald. I cut it short and dyed it blonde (then other shades) in preparation for chemo. It helped destigmatize it for them. "What color should we dye it this week?" I'd ask. By now, they are completely unfazed. Wig, hat, bare head: they don't bat an eye.

But I do much more than give information and marvel at their ability to adapt. I tell them when I'm just feeling too tired or down, and I do let myself cry in front of them. An early-childhood educator advised us to reinforce the saccharine notion that "Everything will be okay." I won't do that. I want them to feel safe and loved and to know that *they* will be okay, but not *everything* will be. I'll assure them that they will be taken care of no matter what, but some things will never be the same. I want to acknowledge this, while still affirming that our family will adapt and recover. How else will they learn what it means to face challenges and deal with them? If we put on a facade of normality— and they would sense all the cracks anyway—we're conveying that it's better to stifle our emotions than communicate them.

All of us parents struggle with the myriad challenges and losses of our complicated lives. We shouldn't underestimate our children's capacity to discuss and process the hard stuff. If we don't let them take risks, we inhibit the development of their capacity for independence. So too, if we don't show them what we feel deeply—pain and grief included—we're not showing them that there's a way to move through these emotions and find your way forward.

Erin Hyman was a writer, editor, and rebbetzin (rabbi's wife) in San Francisco. She died within a year after writing this piece.

A Death in the Family

My father is nearing the end of his life. The doctor is telling us it's a matter of a few weeks, at the most. My six-year-old son is very fond of his grandpa and has developed a ritual of playing checkers and cards with him at our visits (about twice a month). This works well because my dad is restricted to his bed or lounge chair. My four-year-old daughter is less connected to grandpa: there's not much they can do together. But she still likes our visits (I confess that I "sweeten the deal" by getting them ice cream after each one). I should add that their grandmother died when my oldest was an infant, so, to them, she's just a photograph and a few stories.

I don't know if I should prepare my kids for their grandpa's death in advance or wait until it has happened. Either way, how do I help them deal with it, before and after?

Helping your child prepare for, understand, and deal with the death of a close family member is very trying (and thus, this chapter will be longer than the usual), partly because we ourselves, as adults, often feel unprepared and at a loss. You will need to have different strategies for each child. Their bonds with their grandpa are different and their cognitive comprehensions of death at vastly different stages.

Now, before you launch into helping your children, take an emotional inventory of yourself. What's your relationship with your father like? How do you expect to deal with his death? Any lingering hurts and disappointments, especially when unspoken, will complicate your emotional response and may impact how you explain things to your kids. Take stock and get some help, from a close friend, clergy, or a therapist, to clear your path to reconciling with your father's death.

Let's begin with the question of preparation before the anticipated death. For your six-year-old, especially, some time to digest the information that grandpa will die soon will be very helpful. He will need clear explanations of the following points:

1. What do you think death means? Do you believe in an afterlife? Are you an empiricist, feeling the body decomposes (if buried, or turned to ash in cremated—more on that later), and there's nothing *real* left except our love and memories?

2. What will happen *before* Grandpa dies? Briefly describe the body slowing down and shutting down. Tell your son that, at some point soon, Grandpa won't be able to play with him anymore, and after that, he may no longer be able to speak or even show he's aware of your son's presence. You can be somewhat vague about it: "Toward the end, we may not know for sure if Grandpa knows you are there. He may not be able to show it. But we think he'll still feel it in some way."

3. If your father will be hooked up to IVs, ventilators, and such, you need to prepare your son and say something like, "It may look scary or awful, but it's helping him breathe and get his blood to go everywhere inside his body." I would advise not bringing the four-year-old into the room to see that. If possible, remove those temporarily while she's visiting.

4. Next, your kids will want to know what will happen to make Grandpa die. Explain that eventually, the body stops working: Grandpa will stop breathing, his heart will stop pumping blood, and he will be dead. Ask each child what *they* think being dead is like. Listen for the details they imagine and correct any that are wrong. This will also be the moment to talk about the soul if that is in your belief system. You can

say that grandpa's soul, or spirit, or "The person he was in his heart and mind" will go to rest with God. It's a reassuring idea if *you* believe it, but fraught: you may need to answer many more questions about the "mechanics" of the soul's afterlife. Allow yourself to say, "I am not sure. Nobody really knows because people who die can't come back and tell us about what happens."

If an afterlife is not aligned with your beliefs, stick to the facts, and simplify a bit for the younger child. Explain, "After someone dies, his body no longer works, it can't move and can't feel anything. We put the body in a coffin [explain that it's a big wooden box] and bury it in a grave in the cemetery, so everyone can know where it is. A lot of people like to go and visit the grave. It helps them remember all the good things about the person who died and think about how much they miss them. We will do that, too."

If your father will be cremated, I would avoid relaying that information to your four-year-old altogether. Too scary! Your six-year-old is likely to find it hard to handle, as well. Imagining a body in a coffin, safely interred in the earth, is much more palatable than a body burning. For him, you'll need to stress over and over that the body feels nothing after death and allow him to express his dismay. All you need to say is, "Yes, I know it's hard to think of that."

With both kids, but mostly with the four-year-old, be very attentive to the words you and others use, especially any euphemisms about death, such as "going to sleep," "departing," or "going away." All those are activities of normal daily life, which you do not want your kids to confuse with death.

Another common usage to beware of is: "Grandpa died and went to Heaven." I was once called to help a little boy who wouldn't go out of the house after his grandfather died. I finally elicited the reason: he'd been told, "Grandpa went to Heaven." Having heard that Heaven is "up in the sky," he was afraid that if he went outdoors, right under the sky, Grandpa would step on his head.

Another child seemed extremely disturbed after his grandfather died. I managed to gather that he had been told that there would not be a funeral locally because "they sent the body to be buried in New York." He was freaked out asking, "But what about the head?" Can you imagine the pictures he'd painted in his mind? Grandpa's head severed from the body, stuck in a corner somewhere...

Now, what about the funeral? It used to be a given that children did not attend funerals. I think that was and is a mistake. Generally, children from age four or five on (depending on the child) can follow the proceedings and sit through the event. Attending a funeral can help such children integrate that the death is final, everyone is sad, people support each other with hugs and love, and the living go on.

I have mixed feelings about an open casket (something I have personally only experienced once). On the one hand, I see the value of a child seeing a beloved family member for the last time. He can witness that the body is there, in a coffin, but is not alive anymore and cannot move or respond. He can join family members in saying goodbye. However, the common practice of embalming and dressing the body in fine clothes may be a bit confusing, as the dead person looks "perfectly fine," maybe much better than they had in recent weeks or months. So a child might wonder, are they really dead? With a closed coffin, there is not the clear visual of the dead body. Your child may wonder if it's really in there, inside the coffin. You need to assure them that it is. I expect you will do what's right for your family, in line with your traditions and practices, so the key is to prepare your child for what they'll see.

Another very important point is that, if you expect you will be very distraught, you should make sure someone is present to focus on supporting your kids. It can be an aunt or uncle, a preschool teacher, or a familiar babysitter. After the funeral, don't expect your kids to socialize with the guests. It's perfectly fine for the designated adult to take them for a walk, play with them in a separate room in the house or the yard, or serve them a snack.

In the ensuing days, start making a book about Grandpa with each child (use the structure outlined in the "Let's Make a Book About It: My Pet Died" section of this book). Return to the book as often as each child wants to, initiating it once a week for at least a month or two if your child does not bring it up on their own. In the book, include a section about other people who have died that your child is aware of, such as Grandma, and talk about how we remember them.

When a Pet Dies

We have two kids, ages four and six, and a beloved dog. The dog is getting very old and sick, and we can see the end of his life approaching. We want to euthanize him before he is in pain, but we are nervous about how our kids will take it. Should we involve them in the decision? How should we handle the burial? How can we help our kids deal with the death?

The death of a pet is perhaps the most trying experience for young children who are lucky enough to live free of war, crime, serious illness, and poverty. As sad as it'll be for your children, it is actually a gift, as it provides an opportunity to deal with death on a manageable scale. It creates the foundation for responding to death when it comes later in life in grave circumstances.

First, I advise you *not* to involve your children in the decision about if and when to put the dog down. They are not mature enough to weigh the pros and cons and will likely want to prolong the dog's life as long as possible. This is a decision for adults to make (though I could see involving teenage kids), and your job is to present it to your children as final in as supportive a way as possible. That said, I urge you to prepare your kids (especially the older one) by saying that the dog is getting very old (or sick) and will die soon. Give your kids the opportunity for last special things with the dog: a walk in a favorite spot, many doggy treats, taking pictures of your kids hugging the dog, and letting him sleep on their bed.

I advise burying the dog (standing in this section for any pet) and having a funeral. It provides an opportunity for marking the farewell, appropriate crying, and a spot where the body will remain. Think of it as a rehearsal for the death of a family member or friend (hopefully not for years). Your kids may want to use religious language and ceremonies; it's how all of humanity copes with death. When our dog died, mine invented a ritual that reminded me of ancient Egypt: burying him with their most treasured possessions. For my son, age ten, that was a comic book, and for my daughter, age seven, it was a Barbie doll.

After the funeral, make a book with each child. You can use the full-length book at the end of this book or follow these steps:

1. On the first page, paste the child's photo and have her write her name.

2. On page two, put a photo of the whole family.

3. Page three is for a photo/your child's drawing of the dog. Have her write/dictate a description of the dog.

4. Use several pages to write and illustrate (best to have kids draw on every page) the greatest things about the dog, favorite activities together, family dog stories, etc.

5. Save a page to be completed a little later on what was annoying about the dog ("peed on the rug," "ate my homework").

6. Next write down your child's response to the opening sentence: "My dog died, and that makes me feel:" and on the following page/s: "This is what I think about dying," and "What my parents/aunt/teacher/rabbi said about dying." Add other pages along this line: "What books say about dying," "Other things [animals and people] I know that have died," and, finally, "If I could talk to my dog now, I would say."

Let your children set the pace. They may want to do the whole book in one or two intensive sittings or only one page at a time. Your younger child may want to "play funeral" over and over. Encourage this and listen for any exaggerated fears or unrealistic notions. Gently address and correct these at an opportune time.

Some kids bounce back fast, and others nurse their grief for a long time. In either case, the key is for them to know they can ask you any question they might have and come to you for comfort. Hold off on suggesting a new pet for at least a few weeks. Don't rush your kids or yourself.

Moving Is Hard on Kids

We're moving this summer for new jobs and getting closer to most of our family. But we're leaving behind Grandma and many friends. We'll drive across country as the movers depart, hopefully arriving after our stuff does. How should we prepare our kids (ages ten, five, and two) for the move?

Moving is a difficult experience for most kids. Parents easily underestimate how hard it will be, with the excitement, hubbub, and sheer labor involved. Your kids' ages mean you'll face different issues with each one, yet all have a common thread: "How dare you uproot me from my home and friends?"

Adults can't quite grasp that for very small kids, a place you have not been to doesn't exist (maps, photos, videos notwithstanding). Besides, kids' attachment to their surroundings is likely to focus on things you're oblivious to: a crooked curbstone by the driveway, a shiny door handle, a scrawny bush under their window.

Even though they've probably traveled, seen, and tasted more than you did at their age, kids have fewer life experiences than you do now. This gives them little to rely on to cope with moving. With today's electronic "realities," we imagine that we "get" everything. This is particularly illusory with young kids: seeing it on an iPhone or iPad is *not* like being there.

In preparing your kids, start with the toddler, knowing that everything true for them is, in more sophisticated, less obvious ways, also true for the siblings. The younger the child, the smaller the circle of people and things to consider, but don't underestimate your little one's attachments. When my son was almost two, we moved to Los Angeles for a year. He adjusted easily, but when we entered our home one year later, he ran around in a frenzy from one room to the next, shouting, "I am home! I am home!" He remembered not only every object but the *feeling* of being home.

Follow this plan (or use of the "We Are Moving" book at the end of this book):

1. Photograph kids' beds (unless you *can* take them) and rooms, then arrange the furniture and hang the pictures and decorations the same way in the new house (as much as possible).

2. Explain "moving" with pictures of a moving truck, boxes, and details of packing, shipping, and unpacking.

3. Let each child pack some boxes with you, then prepare a bag with their most precious things to take on the drive.

4. Two weeks before the move, start making a book, "We Are Moving" (make your own or use the book included here) for the younger children directing them from page to page. The ten-year-old can make her own book as she wishes.

5. Take the books to preschool and kindergarten for friends and teachers to write or draw in. The teachers may initiate making a "Farewell Book." If not, suggest it.

6. Include a trip diary if you are driving for more than two days.

7. Once you've arrived, add the new home to the book. If your children resist, they are showing you they're still mourning losing their old home. Don't rush it!

8. Over several weeks, add pages with photos and writings about new places and friends.

9. The last page is for your child's "Advice for other kids who have to move."

Now for the ten-year-old. On the face of it, it's easier: ten-year-olds comprehend so much more. But prepare for an avalanche of feelings: a preview of adolescent angst and sulking. Provide any information they want, but remember they'll get more out of doing their own research and setting up social media to stay in touch with their friends. Indirect ways to address their feelings may work best. They'd likely sneer at the idea of making a book, so ask them to help their five-year-old sibling. They'll each get just as much out of it.

Finally, ask Grandma to visit within two months after your move and come back again a few months later.

II. In the Big World: Violence and Injustice

How to Talk About School Shootings and Other Horrors

This was originally written after the Sandy Hook Elementary School massacre. It is horrifying that it remains relevant. How do you explain it to your child?

Talking to Kids Under Age Eight

1. Don't! If at all possible, shield your child. I believe that a big part of parenting is protecting your children from this kind of information. When a horror or disaster strikes, don't listen to the radio or watch TV if your kids are home. Get your updates electronically and delay conversations until kids are asleep.

2. If your child has heard about it, do your best to reassure them, first and foremost, of their safety at home and school (see more below: simplify everything for your child's level).

3. Expect old "stuff" to come up for several weeks: frightening and sad experiences, old anxieties your child had overcome.

Watch for behavioral signs: sleep problems, appetite changes, lethargy, social withdrawal, fear of going to school. All this needs talking and acknowledging, reassurance, and patience. It may also call for modifications in your routines, such as walking your child into her classroom instead of dropping them off at the curb.

From Age Eight to Middle School

Your child is very likely to hear the news, one way or the other. Consider bringing it up yourself so you can shape the information she gets. Key issues:

1. Why? Your child will ask why it happened, why the gunman did it. Obviously, you have to present what you believe. I'll offer my view as one option. Though no expert on this phenomenon, I agree with David Cullen (author of *Columbine*) that the underlying cause is a suicidal depression and rage. I would say: "The man had the worst kind of an illness called depression. It means that he is terribly sad and angry all the time; his thinking and emotions don't work at all like a regular person's." Emphasize how different it is from common sadness and anger. That said, do tell your child that depression affects kids as well. Stress that they should talk to you or any trusted adult if they ever worry about themselves or a friend.

2. Fears: Your child is likely to be afraid of both this and other threats. Tell them: "People get afraid about many things when something terrible like this happens." If they seem really shaken up, offer to help in a concrete way (e.g., sleeping in their room for a few nights).

3. School safety: Assure your child that her school has its own security arrangements. Follow up with the school to get specific information.

4. Helplessness: All of us, kids and adults, feel terrible that there is nothing we can do to make this better for the victims.

Encourage writing a letter to the victims. Let your child know that heartfelt words are all that's needed.

5.   Talk about guns: This is a controversial issue, but even if you are against stricter gun control, you must address it (see the chapter about young kids and guns). With kids over eight or so, emphasize the lethal danger of firearms and their glorification in our culture.

Seventh-Grade and High School Students

Assume that your child has access to all the information you have. All the suggestions above apply, but additional critical points are:

1.   Discussing with your child the complexity of depression and building/strengthening channels of communication whenever your child or one of their friends struggle with it. Talk in specifics about what your child could and should do if they or a friend are experiencing depression or bullying (in or out of cyberspace).

2.   Discuss guns, our gun-intoxicated culture, and the politics of gun control.

3.   Encourage your child to participate in a club/program at school that addresses bullying and violence, or in political action.

While you help your child, be sure to find ways to address your own feelings. Some of the suggestions above— writing to the victims' families, praying for them, and participating in local vigils and political action— will likely help you, too. And, if you can, find a place in your heart or prayers for the surviving family of the gunman. Their lives, too, have been shattered.

Explaining Homelessness and Poverty

I overheard this conversation right between the bank and a popular bakery:

"Mommy, why is the man lying on the street?"

"He... must be tired."

"So why doesn't he go home to take a nap?"

"He doesn't have a home."

"Why?"

"Some people don't have enough money to have a house or an apartment to live in."

"So why doesn't he buy some money from the machine, like we did?"

"To get money from the machine, you have to first give it to the bank."

"Why?"

"It's complicated... Shall we go into the bakery? Do you want a roll or a cookie?"

How would you explain homelessness to young children?

When kids ask a simple question like the child you overheard, they put us in a very uncomfortable spot. First of all, we don't have a good explanation to justify this injustice. Second, the problem of homelessness is complicated, and the solutions tried by most localities inadequate. The child's naïve question reminds us that it ought to be self-evident that every person should have a home. But enough preaching... what should you say (and do)?

Start by engaging your child in a longer conversation rather than changing the subject. Explain the basic facts:

1. Some people don't have enough money to buy or rent a home.

2. There are places called "homeless shelters" where such people can stay, at least for a while, but there are not enough for everyone who needs them. There are shelters for adults who are by themselves and also for families. Support your child if she's outraged that there are kids who don't have a home!

3. The people we see sitting or sleeping on the street usually have a lot of problems "with their feelings and their thinking." This makes it hard for them to stay at one of those shelters or find a job and earn money so they can rent a place to live.

4. Now ask your child what *they* think about that. Expect and encourage expressions of empathy, concern, and anger at

the way things are. Next, tell your child what you do. Do you contribute to a homeless shelter? To broad-based homeless services in your city? To a food bank? If not... get cracking.

You should consider your position on panhandling. Do you give a small amount? Do you refrain because it encourages begging and because the money is often used for alcohol? Are you uncomfortable with either choice? I am.... What I usually do is decline to give money but ask the person if they'd like some pastry from the bakery or a piece of fruit from the grocery store next door. What is your policy? Does your child understand it? Can they see that you care? If not, perhaps you want to consider doing something that will demonstrate your compassion more concretely.

If your child seems really troubled (which you should welcome as an indication of their compassion and sense of justice) take further steps, such as:

1. Volunteer at a family shelter (serving meals, planting a garden, etc.).
2. Have your child make holiday cards for kids in a shelter.
3. Collect books/toys to donate.
4. Volunteer at a Food Bank.
5. Organize your church, synagogue, mosque, or other community group to adopt a shelter or provide housing or meals during the winter months.

This is a great opportunity to talk with your child about how lucky they are to have everything they have, both material and not, and to foster gratitude, which is the foundation of generosity.

Talking About the Holocaust

What do you think about talking to young kids about the Holocaust? Is it totally out of bounds for young children? When is an appropriate time? We have survivors in our extended family, but not in our children's everyday life. What do you advise?

Talking with young kids about the Holocaust requires utmost thoughtfulness and caution. As a general rule, I would *not even broach the subject until middle school.* However, if your child has picked up some information and asks you about it, you need to address it. Pressure to bring up the Holocaust sooner may stem from:

1.   Relatives who are survivors (though they are becoming rarer and rarer) and deeply engaged in your children's lives. Their need to tell their story, your child's curiosity about their childhood, or the number on their forearm may be the initial prompt.

2.   Rather commonly (Jewish) religious school directors want to introduce the topic in the elementary school grades. I believe this is much too young! I can't be sure what the motivations may be; perhaps the teachers want to inculcate the information and awareness before kids leave their school, but I would discourage it.

That said, what do you do if the subject does come up? As with any sensitive topic, ask your child: "What have you heard? What are you wondering about?" (You may find out that she is only wondering if it's a day off from school.) If you learn your child has heard that it is something awful, about killing, gassing, or concentration camps, get to work.

Be especially careful with your choice of words so you do not create a misimpression that we are talking about camps like the summer camp they have or will attend. Take your child's lead in how much they need to know and err on the side of vague: "It was really, really awful." Acknowledge that many, many Jews and other people were killed, but don't go into how.

With young children (preschool to second grade), consider a simple ritual and explanation suggested by my friend and veteran Oscar-worthy early childhood educator, Janet Harris. "During circle or group meeting time, I show the children all different types of candles: birthday candles, Shabbat, Havdalah (End of the Sabbath), etc. I then bring out a *Yahrtzeit* candle (in Jewish tradition, a death anniversary candle) and ask if anyone has ever seen one before. Then I follow the children's lead in a discussion and describe the Yahrtzeit candle as a sad candle." You can do the same at home and ask your child what they might think of for a "sad candle." Follow that by whatever amount of information seems appropriate about when and why adults are sad.

Remember that if you are talking about family members, survivors, or victims, you want to share with your child what their life was like before the Holocaust. Focus on the ordinary aspects of life that she can relate to, such as games they played, what their school was like, who lived in their home, what they ate, how they celebrated holidays, birthdays, and weddings. The point is to help your child imagine these relatives and their lives, to balance the dark shadow of their death. And, of course, acknowledge how sad it is that they died and are not a part of your life.

With middle school children, you should still gauge what they need to know by asking questions first and listening carefully. Provide the information that most of Europe's Jews were killed, that the Nazis were the evilest regime the world had seen, and that people starved and were in forced labor camps. I would still try to avoid the gas chambers and horrors of that level. Some age-appropriate books can help you address the subject.

By the time they reach later middle schools and high school, most children are ready for the historical facts. But even here, I would proceed with caution, especially when it comes to showing photographic images, especially in film. Describe in words what the photos or film will show and ask your child if they want to watch it. Watch together and stop on occasion to talk and process the information.

When Kids Ask about God

We love our synagogue [substitute "church" or "mosque" as fits your faith] *for the traditions, the community, and the special moments marking a passage and taking stock. But we aren't God-fearing people; not even God-believing. I am in the agnostic range; my husband is an atheist. Our five-year-old came back from services this year full of God questions (at least he was paying attention!): Who is God? Why do we talk to Him? Does He ever answer? What does God look like? Where is He? How can He hear us if, as one friend told him, "He is up in the super high skies?"*

We want to be honest about our beliefs, but we don't want to squash his. What do we say?

What a great question! It reminds me of when my son came home from his first day of kindergarten (at a Jewish day school) and asked: "Who is God? And why do they keep talking about him?"

Many thoughtful parents, up-to-date on all child development matters, would rather talk about where babies come from than about God. The babies question has an answer with scientific facts; the God issue is all a matter of belief. Young children can find a lot of comfort in the idea of a loving God watching over them (while for others, it can be scary). It seems like a natural extension of their family experience, of parents protecting and taking care of them. My daughter asked her four-year-old friend what he thinks about God, and he said, "I believe in a daddy, a mommy, and a baby." And mind you, he was a 100 percent Jewish boy!

As with every challenging topic, my suggestion is you start by finding out what your child already knows and thinks, and what and why he wants to know. Let's assume that it is, in your case, related to what your son heard in *shul* (synagogue). Explore it further: Is he wondering if there is someone "up there" watching him? If so, is that reassuring, the idea of someone to protect him? Or is it frightening to think that someone sees his every move and secret thoughts? Or is this really about normal developmental anxieties about his safety or part of a developing scientific understanding that things exist if you can see or measure them?

Second, make it clear early in this conversation that this is a topic where different people have different ideas. Since almost everybody agrees that you cannot see, touch, or measure God (apologies to certain medieval Jewish Kabbalists and Christian theologians), people have different opinions. Explain the difference between a fact and a belief.

Finally, your child will most probably want to know what you believe and is likely to want to agree with you. Stay true to your views without imposing them in a heavy-handed way. I told my son (abbreviated here): "God is an imaginary being that some people believe in and think watches over the world, and some people don't. I don't, but you can believe whatever seems right to you." That may sound dismissive, but "imaginary beings" were totally real to him! Be they superheroes or evil magicians and wicked witches, they lived vividly in his mind. We also discussed other things that you can feel but not see, such as love, pride, or fear.

My daughter, on the other hand, filled me in on her theology without prompting (after that conversation with her friend). She had a whole system worked out: when people died, their bones became telephones through which they communicated with God and the living. The bones served those alive as well: you could talk with the dead through them, even though she knew perfectly well that the bones were buried underground. You could also use them to find out anything you wanted to know and see your relatives and friends who were far away. She later dubbed these "tele-bones." Did she anticipate the iPhone? Did we miss our chance for a patent?

Seriously, though, this conversation is very important! Do leave your child ample room to form his own beliefs, and do present your views in a way that does them justice. If your child shows a lot of curiosity, arrange for him to speak with a rabbi, priest, or imam, preferably one who believes in God (not all do).

PART V: Holidays, Family Celebrations and Extended Family Relationships

I. Holidays

Interfaith Families and Holidays

*W*e are an interfaith family raising our children Jewish, but we also want to nurture their close relationship with their Christian grandparents, who are quite devout. Christmas is, of course, a big deal in the family, and we have always come to Christmas Day Dinner and enjoyed family ties and too much food (they seem very Jewish in that respect). Now that our kids are six and four, we wonder if we should draw a line anywhere about how much Christianity we are comfortable with.

Many Jewish, Muslim, and other non-Christian families in interfaith marriages try to maintain a balance between both religious traditions to which they are heir. Christmas is, of course, the predominant Christian holiday, but there may be others where you may wonder how to negotiate the dose of Christianity your kids get. Easter comes to mind for the second-place spot (see the chapter on Easter), but if your in-laws are devout, they might want to take your children to church for a Sunday Mass, the special days during Lent, even Pentecost (time to go to Wikipedia to learn more).

Before we get into the details of rituals and customs, you need to consider the larger question: have your parents-in-law truly accepted that your children are being raised Jewish (or another religion)? Or is there some lingering hope and subtle (or not) efforts to influence, even convert, them? The latter is unlikely, but you need to keep it in the back of your mind. If it feels like some part of the Christian celebration the grandparents want your children to enjoy is a little too seductive, you are probably reacting to a covert (and probably unconscious) attempt to influence them. If an honest conversation about this seems feasible, I'd go for it. But a delicate balancing and polite drawing of the lines may be a better path for avoiding all-out family conflict.

As for specifics: where you draw the line depends very much on your level of comfort or discomfort with an indoor tree, a jolly fat man sliding down the chimney, or a bunny that leaves chocolate eggs all around the lawn. Personally, I would be perfectly comfortable with telling your kids that they are getting Christmas presents from their grandparents because "Grandma and Grandpa are Christian. They celebrate Christmas, and giving presents is a big part of it." I would ask the grandparents not to get Santa all mixed up in this. I would think the idea of Santa slithering through the chimney into the house when you are asleep is rather unsettling.

Talk with the grandparents about presenting the birth-of-Jesus story in a way that is palatable to you, e.g., a very special baby who grows up to be a great leader and teacher, without the immaculate-conception and Son-of-God parts. I would certainly ban the crucifixion and resurrection for now, but you knew that, right?

If you are okay with your children going to Mass with their grandparents (Midnight Mass or Sunday), I would:

1. Make sure there's not a graphic crucifix in the church (the kind with a very dead-looking Jesus and bleeding wounds).

2. Take them to synagogues (or mosque if you are Muslim) as
    well, so they experience the parallel in a Jewish (or Muslim)
    setting.

I am reminded of when my son was about three years old and
our very close friends had a baby and invited us to the baptism. It
was going to be a long service, so they suggested he go with their
son to the children's service. The boys came back with huge smiles,
each wearing a hand-made paper crown on which the teacher had
neatly printed: "Jesus Is My King." Our friends were mortified! They
fell over themselves with apologies. And we? We chuckled and have
retold the story every time we have been together.

Too Many Presents

*Chanukah and Christmas are nearing, and we are blessed with a
large extended family. We are a bit worried about CPO: Chanukah/
Christmas Presents Overdose. Last year our son was almost two and
seemed overwhelmed. I'm afraid he disappointed many relatives by
being more interested in the boxes than in the presents. Advice?*

Glad you have the presence of mind to realize you should make
a "presents response plan" for handling the anticipated avalanche
of gifts. Some years, Chanukah comes well before Christmas. This
provides a nice opportunity to differentiate between the two holidays,
as well as, should the pile of presents be excessive, donating some
(at least any duplicates) to holiday toy drives (usually conducted by
your local fire department).

Let me begin with a personal experience. When my daughter
was around your son's age, a family in her preschool invited us to
their Christmas Day lunch. It was one of those years when Chanukah
and Christmas were more than two weeks apart, so we thought
there would be no "Christmas Confusion/Christmas Envy" issue.
We arrived in the late morning to find the family huddled rather
glumly in the living room. Their little boy was, in fact, crying his

eyes out. "What's wrong?" I asked the distraught parents. "He is crying because he doesn't know what to do with so many presents. He doesn't know how to choose which ones to open." He was not amenable, the mother went on, to any constructive suggestions from either his parents or his older sister.

I am sure you have seen similar scenes at birthday parties. The four-year-old "Birthday Boy," already ratcheted up to his maximum tolerance with excitement and sugar, starts opening the presents and soon falls apart. The other kids are unhappy too because all each guest wants to see is the birthday boy opening *their* present. Sitting patiently through ten others is not in their repertoire.

Presumably, family members who have brought presents have a longer attention span. Still, even mature adults want to have their gift appreciated, and at least some young children are very attuned to these expectations and feel a lot of pressure. My preferred guideline for birthday parties (and Chanukah parties) is a balanced equation of age-guests-gifts. In other words, a four-year-old has four guests at his birthday party and gets four presents. Think that sounds too limiting for Chanukah? Then double it, so your four-year-old gets eight presents in all (one for each day).

This also connects to the issues I raised in my last column about cultivating thankfulness in children. Too many presents undermine that. How much thankfulness can you feel? This is something you can address in a gradual way through "thank you" cards. Wait to write each until *after* your child has had a chance to play with or use the gift. For example, if your child got a painting easel set from his grandparents, have him use it to make a painting for them and others in the family. A card that accompanies such a painting with the note "I painted this picture with the paints and easel that you gave me!" means much more to both your child and the grandparents than a bought (or even hand-made) generic "thank-you" card.

Presents and thank-you cards aside, I urge you strongly to plan several other family activities for Chanukah, focused not on gifts but instead on fun times together and generosity toward others. An additional benefit of the gap between Christmas and Chanukah when this occurs: you can find a volunteer opportunity for Christmas Day or the week before, such as serving Christmas dinner at a homeless shelter or donating and/or wrapping gifts for needy kids.

If your family is an interfaith one and you celebrate both holidays, you'll have a double dose of presents. Again, think about a reasonable limit on how many gifts your child gets and balance it with presents to be given.

Christmas Envy

Help! How do we help our kids rejoice (and be satisfied) in celebrating Chanukah when we're surrounded by Christmas everywhere we go?

Let's face it, for young children, Chanukah does not hold a candle to Christmas. A floor-to-ceiling tree with all the ornaments versus your menorah (even if it's a beautiful one)? A jolly bearded man sliding down the chimney with a sack of presents versus a top that spins and falls of one of four letters? A pile of gift boxes you can swim in versus a present each of eight nights? Okay, *maybe* Chanukah has a chance on the eight-days-of-presents end, but barely...

By now I suspect your anxiety level is rising: what's a Jew to do? In a family where both parents are Jewish? In an interfaith marriage? When one parent is a convert, but the grandparents still want to celebrate Christmas, or at least give their grandkids Christmas presents (see more in the previous chapter on "Interfaith Families and the Holidays")?

First, and most importantly, don't panic and don't overreact. If "Christmas envy" becomes a focus of tremendous family pressure, whatever you say or do will, inevitably, communicate to your child that Christmas is a huge deal. Instead, you want to let your child know that it's a nice thing that other people do. In a way, the simple explanation like: "Only Christians celebrate Christmas," makes perfect sense to young children. It would be easier to close the loop of "We are Jews, and we celebrate Chanukah" if it were called "Jewnukkah," but I don't see that happening. So, use these simple suggestions as a start to address Christmas:

1. Answer your children's questions honestly, simply, and nonchalantly. When they ask, "How come we don't have Christmas?" don't cover the 4,000 years of Jewish history. Simply say, "Christians celebrate Christmas. We are Jewish, so we don't." Then leave an opening for your children to tell you what's on their mind. Is it envy of their friends in preschool talking about presents? Is it fears about "Santa Claws" slipping into your house when you are asleep? Did they hear something worrisome about the "naughty and nice" (which does plug right into six-year-olds' nascent conscience and sense of justice)? Answer each question or worry right to the point, without unnecessary elaborations.

2. Arrange with friends or neighbors who celebrate Christmas for your children to come over a few days before Christmas to help them decorate their tree. Emphasize to them that they are doing a nice thing for their friends/neighbors. Have them bring small presents that you wrap together for the neighbors' children *and* ask the neighbors to have small presents waiting for your kids, in turn. They can open it as soon as you get home, and you can say, "Lucky you, you don't have to wait till Christmas morning." This applies, of course, to your own family members who celebrate Christmas: do it at their homes.

3. Find an activity to do as a family that emphasizes helping people, whether they celebrate Chanukah (such as delivering food to home-bound seniors in the Jewish community) or Christmas (participating in a local toy drive or serving Christmas Day dinner at a church or shelter). Whatever you

pick, have your children make their own holiday cards to add to the delivery.

4. Within your family, emphasize *making* over buying. Children (and adults, too!) get much more meaning and pleasure from making gifts than from buying them. Grandparents and aunts and uncles are, of course, the best recipients of these creations.

5. In celebrating the eight days of Chanukah, plan on doing something special together each night, as a family and with friends, over a parade of presents. One novel idea that may bring wonderful surprises is a night of "doing nothing." It's a family evening together using no gadgets (not even books!) to entertain yourself and your children. You'll be amazed by the creativity and fun!

6. Consider joining the now cherished-by-many "Jewish Christmas" tradition of a movie and Chinese dinner. Or make up your own ritual to celebrate that the stores are all closed, the streets are nearly empty and, almost everyone is off work.

If your family members like grandparents, in-laws, or cousins celebrate Christmas, *and* you have good relations and easy communication, ask them to tone things down in the tender years of three to five. But if this will be a bone of contention, just bite your tongue. Think up your own family's way to balance Chanukah and Christmas. My friends in Vermont, he Jewish, she Christian, did just that. On Christmas Eve, they would bundle up their four small children and go into their own woods, cut a small tree, and haul it home on their sled. They decorated it with homemade ornaments and put the presents under it. Christmas day, everyone opened them. The next morning, they all got up very early and, with equal pomp and circumstance, hauled the tree out and heaved it onto the garbage in a "Tossing of the Tree" ritual.

"Christmas envy" or not, I hope you find your own pleasures and peace in this sometimes-fraught season.

Purim Problems:
What's Appropriate for Young Children?

Our kids attend a Jewish day school and are very excited about Purim. They love the costumes and parties. But this year, I am worried: my daughter is in second grade and may well hear the full story, including the genocidal parts: first the threat against the Jews, then the Jews' pre-emptive killing of their neighbors. Even if they skip it in school, I know she'll notice it at the Megillah reading in shul. Furthermore, she loves to play "school" with her four-year-old brother, so I worry she'll pass it on to him, too. What should we do?

Glad you raised this issue! It will come up again at Passover with the plagues, especially the killing of the firstborn and the drowning of the Egyptians (see the chapter on that). I share your view that parts of the Purim story in the Book of Esther are too frightening and troubling for young children. I recommend shielding kids from this at least until fourth grade. By then, they are equipped to separate our reality and values from those we find in ancient societies, the Bible included.

First, let's see if you can create a "buffer zone" for your kids. Discuss this with her teachers at school and clergy at shul. Suggest planning a special kids' activity, say a Purim Treasure Hunt, scheduled precisely during the reading of the bloodiest passages. Kids get antsy anyway during the lengthy reading, though they sure love the noisemaking at Haman's name.

If, nevertheless, your daughter does hear the gruesome parts, you'll need an in-depth conversation with her. There are various ways to try to explain to young children how different things were in ancient times, though, to be honest, I think they don't truly get it (not to mention the many places in the world today where things are just as violent and gruesome). Make it very concrete: first things that are the same: families, parents loving their children, kids enjoying play. Now introduce those things that are different: no TV, no cars or phones, and no school for children. Also, not much playtime. Tell her that kids her age already worked very hard to help their family survive—carrying water, caring for their younger siblings, gathering wood for the fire—and ask her if she can think of other differences. Next, move to the issue at hand: even though people believed in goodness and justice (give examples), they also accepted, more than *we* do today, racism, national hatred, violence, and vengeance.

Don't overdo it: listen more than you talk. Ask what *she* thinks. I expect she'll express horror that people would want to kill the Jews and also that the Jews would "kill them back." Perfect! Tell her, "I am so happy you don't want anyone to be killed, and I agree with you. But, sadly, it happened then, and it still happens in some places in the world today." Reassure her that it's *not* something that happens here; that we are lucky to live in a kinder and safer world (and pray that this is true...). Ask her to write and decorate her own Megillah with her ideas for a more peaceful ending. Use it to read at home and have her" teach it" to her brother.

Both the Purim and Passover stories are traditionally read as narratives of Jewish triumph, but you (and all of us) can use them as opportunities to teach empathy and nonviolence. After you discuss alternative ways that these Biblical stories could be told, ask your kids to think of concrete ways to practice these values in their everyday life.

Now, back to the fun: costumes, parades, and parties. This is a wonderful opportunity to have fun together as a family. To make it more enjoyable and meaningful for your kids, try to:

1. Let them choose not only their costumes but yours as well. A "family costume" such as "Goldilocks and the Three Bears" can be a big hit.
2. Make at least part of the costume together: a hat, crown, sword, or basket.
3. Put on skits at home wearing the costumes.

Don't forget that very young children (under three-and-a-half) are easily frightened by the sudden transformation of a familiar face with a mask or costume. They may, at the last minute, refuse to put on the costume over which you've lovingly labored. Try preempting this by rehearsing in advance, repeatedly putting the mask or costume on and taking it off in front of the mirror.

Easter: Explaining the Crucifixion and Resurrection

Our four-year-old loves Easter: decorating the eggs, the bunnies, the egg hunt, and the chocolate, of course. We've expanded to talking about spring and how after the plants in our garden turn brown and wilt (I've been avoiding the word "die") in winter, they come back in spring with beautiful flowers like daffodils and crocuses. But I'm dreading Easter: my son is sure to ask me more pointed questions this year about the crucifixion and the resurrection. He's already asked about the Jesus on the cross in our church, and, I admit, I finessed it by saying, "He's hanging up on the cross so he can watch over us and send us his love." When my son asked, "Doesn't it hurt him?" and "Isn't he cold without any clothes?" I said, "This is a sculpture of Jesus; it doesn't feel pain or cold." But what am I going to say when he asks about "the real Jesus?"

Oh, my, you're in a tough spot. Full disclosure: I am Jewish, so I haven't had to struggle with this problem personally. Perhaps I should advise you to talk to your clergy instead of asking me. That said, let me try to offer some guidelines that, hopefully, will help you calibrate what you say to your child's level of understanding.

First of all, you need to ask yourself what exactly *you* believe. Do you understand the biblical story as literal truth and, thus, believe in miracles? Or, do you take it more as a symbolic story (regardless of the question of the historical figure of Jesus) and focus on the concepts underlying the story? Whichever it is (it may be some other formulation: these are just over-simplified options), you need to convey to your child what you believe. Once your child is school-age and encounters kids from different backgrounds, religious and otherwise, you need to equip him to understand that not everyone (of course, not even all Christians) believes in the same story and ideas.

Now for the developmental issues:

For a child under age four, I would only present the fun aspects: egg hunt, hopping bunnies, and blooming daffodils. Now, by age four, most lucky children (though not all) have encountered death in manageable proportions: a dead bird on the pavement, a dead beetle in the grass. Some children, of course, have faced more grave situations, from the death of a pet to the death of a family member. Assuming you addressed those at the time, this is your starting point.

You can explain that Jesus died too, but not like other people or animals. Because he was "God," "the Son of God," "Magical" (whichever you're most comfortable with), he only died for three days. Then he came back to life and went out into the world to give all of us all his love. His love is also very special: it is as big as the whole world; it's like a hug that everyone can feel at the same time.

I would stay away from the details of the crucifixion for as long as possible, but eventually, your child will ask. Maybe he will have seen a painting, a crucifix at church, or heard the words "crucified" and "Jesus died for our sins" in conversation or the liturgy. I would explain that this happened a really, really long time ago when some rulers (you might add, "like some kings and queens in fairytales") were really cruel and punished people by hanging them on a huge wooden cross. Those punished people would stay there until they died. If your child presses (and only if he presses!), you'll have to mention the nails and say: "It was the worst thing to do! We certainly don't do it anymore." (How I wish I could say that about the whole world...)

Instead of the concept of dying for our sins, I would explain that suffering on the cross made Jesus feel the hurt and sadness that anyone in the world feels. "So," you might say (if it aligns with your belief), "when you get hurt or feel really sad, Jesus understands how you feel. You can think about that and about how much Jesus loves you, and that might help you feel better."

Be sure to emphasize that, even though Jesus was punished, he did *not* do anything wrong. On the contrary, he was always kind and helped people (this part is easy!). But the rulers of the day were mean and did not like him because he said that kindness and love were more important than their rules. Encourage conversation: Was that right? Ask your child what they think the rulers should have done if they didn't like what Jesus was teaching people. Support their protest of the injustice and outrage (I hope!) at what was done to Jesus.

Now, as to the resurrection: if you have taught your child that miracles do or, at least, did happen, you can deploy that concept here. The resurrection was a miracle. But be sure to make it clear that this was a very special miracle that happened only for Jesus because he was not a regular person. It does not happen to regular people, or nowadays. If you firmly believe in the end-of-days resurrection of all, try to explain it to your child in a way that won't make him think that his deceased grandma is coming back soon. You can explain it a different way, without the miracle, by saying that you feel the love of Jesus in your heart, so, to you, that means Jesus is still alive. Or frame it as a story that helps us feel less sad when someone dies, or other bad things happen.

As your child grows and matures, you can get into more details, both historical and theological. You can offer your view, but realize that your child is likely to struggle with making sense of it for himself, with different levels of nuance and sophistication as befits his cognitive development. And it's fine for you to say about some of this, "I feel this very deeply; I believe in it, even if I may not be able to explain exactly how it works. That's okay for me and could be for you, too, but it's up to you. A lot of things in life take a very long time to really understand."

The Ten Scariest Things in the Passover Seder

Our family holds a big Passover Seder, and we encourage our children to participate actively and listen to the readings. We also often add biblical passages that describe in story-form the slavery in Egypt and the Exodus. Now that my daughter is five and has a longer

attention span, I am concerned. What do I do about the violent and
scary parts of the story? And then there's leaving the front door open
for Elijah: that would seem a little freaky to a five-year-old, too, don't
you think?

Yes, the Passover story has many passages that can unsettle
young children. Nevertheless, Passover is my favorite family holiday
(as it is to many other Jewish families as well) and has great moments
and lessons for small kids. There is a lot to consider, so I'll divide this
into two parts. Part I will address passages actually in the Haggadah
and recited at the Seder. Part II will address parts of the Passover
story not actually in the Haggadah but often told at home, at nursery
school, and in children's books. Here are the highlights:

1. The wicked son: who hasn't groaned when reading this? How
   can you be comfortable defining a child as "wicked" and then
   "setting his teeth on edge?" I would discuss this by emphasizing
   the pedagogy we embrace today, saying it is the actions that
   are wicked, not the person. Since we don't exactly know what
   the recommended dental assault is, you can ask your kids for
   their ideas: what should you do when someone asks questions
   clearly intended to be mean and hurtful?

2. Opening the door to Elijah: what could possibly be wrong
   with this lovely custom? Well, when my daughter was four,
   she freaked out at the idea of an invisible man coming
   through the open door and drinking our wine. Between four
   and five, many kids often grow preoccupied with worries
   about their safety. They usually express this with questions
   and games about robbers and kidnappers. They can fear
   about abductions and strangers (especially, unfortunately,
   due to the ill-conceived, yet popular, strategies to "stranger-
   proof" your child: see the chapter on "Fear of Strangers").
   You can either omit this part or be very clear that this is a
   pretend game and that no one will actually enter the house
   or drink the wine. Mark where the wine is on the glass with

a piece of tape, and show your child at the end of the meal that the same amount is still in the glass.

3. "Pour out thy wrath on the nations": during the ritual of opening the door to Elijah, we read the most vengeance-filled passage of the Seder. Kids under five would probably have no idea what "wrath" means and not bother to ask. But if they do, and for older kids who sort of understand, be ready to discuss revenge: why it is such a universal human emotion and why we resist it and replace it with justice.

4. The ten plagues: you are still in the "wrath on the nations" quagmire. Some of the plagues can be entertaining and make the recitation fun, as in the case of the Midrash (commentary) that Exodus says "frog," in the singular, not frogs in the plural, because there was actually one gigantic frog that sat on the Nile and covered all of Egypt. At our Seder, each person has two small plastic frogs on their plate, which they may throw at others during "Frogs." But then you get to "killing the firstborn." There is no way to make this pretty, so discussion and questioning is the way to go.

5. Pharaoh's decree to kill Jewish baby boys: a similarly terrifying idea for a young child, even if she is a girl! Pre-empt the shock with an explanation *you* are comfortable with about evil. For a child under four, it might be something like: "In stories, we make someone who is bad *so bad* that you can't even imagine it." For older children, there's not much you can say beyond acknowledging this horrifying decree as part of human history, Jewish and not, which we must decry and fight.

6. Baby Moses on the Nile: abandoning a newborn baby in a little basket on the Nile is another frightening idea. Emphasize here that it was to protect him and that his big sister (accentuate "big") was watching him the whole time and made sure a good person found him and took good care

of him. You might add: "But, of course, this is a *very* old story. Today parents would never leave their babies like that."

7. "We were slaves:" very young children would not understand what slavery is. A simple explanation suffices: it's when a person works for someone else and has to do everything he says and can't go anywhere or do anything she wants to. Then ask your child how she would feel if she were a slave, and what could she do about it. For children over five, go beyond that: in a gentle way, tell them that even today, there are people enslaved, though slavery is outlawed. (Use your own examples.)

8. Moses kills the Egyptian: Moses, paragon of justice, kills a man, and we just gloss over it and move on with the story! Here is your opportunity to engage your child in a discussion of what he would do if he saw someone hurting another person. Bring it down to his reality: hitting, name-calling, excluding a friend from play. Then circle back to Moses: what could he have done instead, given no justice system to turn to?

9. Drowning of the Egyptians: we're back to the discussion of revenge in the Purim story. Remember the *midrash* about God chastising the angels for cheering: "My creations are drowning, and you are celebrating?" Use it here and ask your child who she thinks is right, God or the angels.

10. Not finding the Afikomen (a third of a matzah hidden until the end of the Passover meal): traditionally, the child who finds it barters it for a prize with the person leading the Seder. But what if they don't find it? And what if there are other young kids at your Seder? For children under age five, losing is very hard. Who wants a heartbroken, sobbing child at the Seder? In our house, we solved this by having a "mini-afikomen" for each of the kids, hidden in an area of the house reserved for them. This allowed us to adjust the difficulty of finding the afikomen to each child's age. And, of course, everyone got prizes!

By now, you may be more anxious about the whole thing than you were before you started reading this. Understood. I suggest you prepare by reviewing the Haggadah before the Seder. If you are a traditionalist and will read every word, plan your explanations and go over some of the topics before the Seder, with ample time for discussion. If you are loose with things, either omit some sections or send the kids to another room at the right moment to prepare a skit of their own about the Passover story. We've had great fun with those, including "Exodus: The Video Game" and "Moses vs. Pharaoh: The WWF [World Wrestling Federation] Championship."

Now to the more practical considerations such as sitting still for soooooo long, singing the *Mah Nishtanah* ("How Is this Night Different than All Other Nights"), etc. Depending on the length of your Seder, this could be your biggest challenge. Be creative with any of the following:

1. A substantial pre-Seder snack.
2. Coloring books (or try coloring on matzahs with thick markers: fun but a lot of crumbs!).
3. A break from the table: take the kids to do a little romping in another room related to the Seder, reenacting *B'nai Yisrael* (the Children of Israel) packing and crossing the Red Sea and preparing a skit for everyone.
4. Design a simple Passover Quiz Show or a huge Exodus "Shoots and Ladders" game on butcher paper taped on the floor.

About singing the Mah Nishtanah: Some kids love the limelight while others find it terrifying. Gauge what's good for your child. Not ready for a solo performance? Have all the kids present do it together. Only one child present? Try a duet by the youngest and oldest at the table.

Finally, a word about cleanup. For kids, cleanup can actually be one of the best parts, that is, if they are still awake (consider starting your Seder early so that it's over before their bedtime). Make it fun and use it as a great opportunity to model cleaning up after yourself. If the

Seder is over really late, sacrifice whatever cleanliness OCD you may have for the educational value of cleaning together the next morning.

Scared Since Halloween

Oy, I've had it with monsters and would like to abolish Halloween! Three weeks since Halloween and my three-and-a-half-year-old son is still terrified. I am not exaggerating. He not only talks about being afraid of monsters, zombies, and ghouls, he literally shakes in his room at bedtime. He's also been waking up scared in the middle of the night, and we must sit with him until he calms down and goes back to sleep.

We've been alternating between taking it seriously and assuring him we'll protect him and dismissing it by saying, "There's no such thing as monsters." We may have made it worse with inconsistency, but one minute he gets that there are no such beings and this approach works, then the next one, he's trembling in fear. I wish I could outlaw Halloween, but, short of that, do you have any suggestions?

The lingering shadow of Halloween is a widespread phenomenon, especially when it falls in that in-between period in your child's life (usually ages three to four) when reality as we know it is not yet firmly established in his mind. Not that older kids (or many adults for that matter) cannot be frightened out of their wits by monsters and other imaginary beings, but they have more tools to reassure themselves that these creatures can't really hurt them.

Let's begin by making a vital distinction between the OBJECT of fear and the FEELING of fear. While the former is not real, and you can say it, explain it, try to prove it by material observation and reasoning, the latter— the *emotion of fear*— is 100 percent real. You need first to help your child cope with how it feels to be afraid (this is true at all ages). Draw up a list of things he can do when he's afraid, including telling you, getting a hug from you, or singing a "Brave Song." Make sure the list includes some things he can do on his own.

At your child's age, there are additional measures you can take that capitalize on his exact vulnerability: his inability to distinguish clearly between reality and fantasy. He is developmentally in the stage we call "magical thinking," which means he believes that what he conjures up in his mind is real. He can hold on the belief that he might be able to fly one day, if only he gets the right cape, powder, or incantation. In the same way, he would believe (at your suggestion) that he could chase away the monsters with a magic wand, a secret word, or an "anti-monster spray."

Here's a simple plan:

1. Start by telling him you can see he's scared: the feeling is real. Talk about the feelings, ask if he can draw them, and add where and how it feels in his body.

2. Reiterate that monsters are not real, but don't dwell on that.

3. Make a poster together, writing, "No Monsters Allowed in This House!" Read it out loud to him and decorate together with colors, stickers, glitter: anything *he* thinks will scare away monsters (even garlic cloves if he's heard of that). Hang the poster on the door to his room and show it to everyone in the family and visitors. Sending a photo of him standing next to it with a brave look on his face to grandparents and aunts and uncles will add to its power.

4. Give him a flashlight or spray bottle (there's actually a company that makes "Monster Defense Brave Spray") to shoo away monsters.

5. Conduct a "Monster Survey" of his room each night before bedtime, assuring it's free of any scary creatures.

6. Let him sleep with the light on.

7. Give him a fierce-looking stuffed animal such as a lion, T-Rex, or bear (let him pick!) as his nighttime companion. Superman PJs may help too.

8. If the middle-of-the-night waking persists, put a mattress on the floor and tell him you'll sleep in his room for a few nights

to help him not be afraid. Say, "I'll be here all night, so you don't need to wake up." If he does, reassure him immediately.

With your benign presence and reassurance, some of these magical elements, and a bit more time, you should be out of "Cape Fear" very soon.

Thanksgiving: How Do You Get from "Say Thank You" to Genuine Gratitude?

Thanksgiving's coming, and we wonder how to teach our four-year-old daughter to be genuinely thankful and appreciative, not just say what she knows we want to hear. We often debate with ourselves whether the typical "What's the magic word?" really teaches anything more than parroting.

There are two interrelated issues here:

1. Teaching children proper manners.
2. Inculcating genuine gratitude.

Let's address them in this order. I am not a fan of the common, overly cutesy prompt: "What's the magic word?" but I do support what stands behind it: the idea that you have to teach young children manners and respect. I don't think that politeness is something that flows naturally out of kids' hearts and mouths. Of course, the primary mode for teaching manners is modeling, but explicit instructions are valuable as well.

Rather than "What's the magic word," say, "How do you ask politely?" or "How did Daddy teach you to ask for things?" Be sure to model "Please, thank you, you are welcome," etc., in your own behavior. That's what will ultimately make these words stick.

Now for a related and often more perplexing issue: what about making your child say "I am sorry" when she has done something unacceptable, especially hurting another child? Here, some child development experts (and parents) argue that a child should only say she is sorry when she is, indeed, sorry. But genuine remorse in the early years happens only a small fraction of the time. Empathy, guilt, and principles of ethical behavior are slow-growth propositions. Apologizing when you don't mean it, goes this view, is worthless emotionally and does not promote the development of true empathy.

Well, I am on the other side here. I do believe that saying you are sorry is an essential part of polite, "civilized" behavior. "*Derekh eretz* preceded [even] the Torah," to quote the Talmud, or "We're living in a society here," to quote *Seinfeld* (my other "Scripture"). It takes young children a long time to develop genuine empathy and remorse. They need to learn earlier on that we do not approve of the behavior in question and that we expect an apology.

Where I would draw the line is in pressing a child to "Say it like you mean it." That really won't work and won't make sense to her either. Generally, it's a good idea to require your child to do only things you can enforce, thus "Stay in your bed," rather than "Go to sleep, already!" Instead, once a child has "performed" the apology, I would encourage, but not require, a concrete act of empathy. For example, if a child has bitten another (very common!), then after having them say they are sorry, send them to bring an ice pack for the bitten child. If a child has snatched a toy from another and pushed them in the process, then after their "sorry," have them give back the toy *and* bring the other child a stuffed animal to hug.

Now to genuine gratitude. Let's be honest: this is an area where most of us can aspire to advance and improve. It's so much easier to kvetch! And it's also so much easier to be angry, envious, entitled, and resentful. With a young child, it's important to go light, specific, and slow in inculcating gratitude. The key is to be concrete. So, you might say: "I am so thankful for this card from my friend because it cheers me up," or "I appreciate that you helped me clean up because we finished faster and now we can read a story." It's the cause and effect between action and the impact on you (or others) that models being grateful. Showing appreciation for ordinary things your child does is where you start. But don't overdo it! Don't thank her every time she lifts her finger to do the tiniest thing to be helpful or cooperative. Gradually raise the bar for what you consider kindness, consideration, and cooperation.

At the Thanksgiving table, many families ask each person to name one thing for which they are thankful. Unless your child loves the spotlight, it's best to prepare so she can offer something meaningful, either in rehearsed words or a picture she has drawn in advance.

Shul Shenanigans

Our three-year-old son loves going to shul [synagogue: substitute "church," "mosque," or "community hall" to fit your situation]. *But over the past months, we have realized this love does not flow from his deeply religious nature, but from the chance to run wild with "The Gang of Four": a small group of four-year-old boys. Our shul is very kid-friendly and has a kids' program for part of the service, but recently we (along with the other parents of this group) have been asked to keep our kids quietly at our side. When we tell our son that he has to stay with us, he throws a huge tantrum. We are on the verge of a moratorium on Shabbat at shul, but (A.) we don't want to miss it (we love shul too!) and (B.) we don't want to give him that kind of power. What shall we do?*

As you have seen, neither parents nor God will trump a group of four-year-old boys in the heart of a three-year-old. That said, you want to harness his passion in the service of fostering a lifelong love for shul and the Shabbat. The question is how to allow enough of the four-year-old-joy-of-mayhem to motivate him while keeping his behavior within reasonable bounds.

Let's begin by acknowledging that many members of the shul are probably thankful someone intervened. As the parents of adorable babies and toddlers, we sometimes forget how others may see them and their antics. Consider coordinating with the other parents of this group to provide a longer children's program, with the parents helping supervise.

That said, it is important to have your son join you for the service for at least a portion, so he can gradually master both the prayers and appropriate decorum. Start by practicing at home until he has memorized a certain section in the service, say ten minutes, including words, melodies, and the getting up and sitting down.

Next, bring him in for that portion and then have him go out to play, preferably with some of his friends. After twenty minutes of play and a short rest, rejoin the service together. Take ten more minutes of focused participation with appropriate behavior. Praise him for it (in moderation) and go outside again for playing. These breaks for outside play will help him build up his stamina. Remember he is likely to need a snack well before the *kiddush* (blessing of the wine and, in most synagogues, a buffet lunch), but you knew that, right?

Swift reaction if he throws a tantrum is key, whether you are inside in the midst of the service or outside during playtime. Immediately pick him up and walk out/away. Keep conversation to a minimum, e.g., "This is not okay!" or "No yelling in shul." Find a quiet spot to sit and talk him down (far enough so people inside won't be bothered by continued screaming). You probably know by now what works with your son. Some kids react well if you speak to them in a calm, firm voice: "You need to stop screaming. Then we can talk about it," or "I can see how upset you are, but you can't scream like that in shul. When you calm down, we can go back in." Some children escalate with each comment you make. If that's your kid, just hold him and wait it out.

With the tantrum over, focus on simple "problem solving" for re-entering shul: "If you are ready to go back in, we can. But remember you have to stay quietly with Mommy and Daddy." Go in gingerly (I suggest the back rows for this "training" period), holding your child in your arms or kneeling down to his level. Whisper in his ear: "You are doing a good job being quiet. Very nice."

After five minutes, check with him if he wants to stay longer or needs a break. Your goal is a successful period of appropriate behavior inside, even if it's only a few minutes. It's much easier to build up from brief successes than undo the negative impact of longer periods that end in meltdowns. But remember, sometimes the best response is to go straight home.

Consistency, firm but undramatic responses to tantrums, and a modicum of praise for good behavior will help your child improve quickly. And, since you are in shul... you might as well add a prayer.

II. Family Celebrations and Relationships

Attending a Gay Wedding

We are invited to my cousin's wedding, our first-ever gay wedding. My kids, ages six and eight, are included, and therein lies my dilemma. I love Mira [fictitious name], *and my kids adore her, so we'd like to attend as a family. However, we are members of a tight-knit, socially conservative community in the Midwest. I know you're in the Bay Area, where LGBT weddings are common, but they're not here in Middle America or our small community. I'll be putting my kids in a very awkward situation. I certainly don't want them to feel they have to keep the wedding a secret, yet I don't think they are sophisticated enough to understand they shouldn't mention the two brides. I don't want to be the center of a controversy in our community; our family doesn't need that kind of attention.*

You are right: here in the San Francisco Bay Area, your dilemma is mostly a thing of the past (at least I hope so). Yet your questions are important, both regarding the specific circumstances and, in general, about putting kids in complex, awkward situations.

Let me begin with my personal experience: my family's first invitation to a gay wedding, over thirty years ago. My kids were about the same age as yours, and they, too, were invited. It was quintessentially Bay Area: not only because it was one of the first Jewish LGBT weddings anywhere, but also because of where it was held: a first-growth redwood grove, which meant an informal ambiance. We told our kids about the wedding invitation (actually a rare thing for them) and that they should know it was two men getting married. My son, at the age when he cared about social conventions, passed. My daughter was ecstatic. At five years old, she was deep into her infatuation-obsession with brides.

We got there early at her insistence, so we'd get seats up front. Flute notes wafted up between the sequoias, and the couple marched down the aisle, dressed in beautiful matching linen suits. My daughter stared; her face fell. "Where's the dress?!"

Shortly after the disappointment, she drew this picture of our wedding, demonstrating the centrality of the dress.

All of this is to say that what this wedding will mean to your kids depends on their expectations, and, of course, on how you handle the explanations. First of all, I urge you to attend the wedding, not just for your cousin's and family's sake, but for your kids. What would you say to them if they asked, now or in years to come, why you didn't attend? Any explanation you might conjure up, short of a lie, would put you in a bad light.

Living in a small, tight-knit conservative community, I imagine your kids have attended several weddings already, so listen for their expectations. Tell them about Mira's wedding and casually mention that her "groom" is a woman. If your kids have met Mira's partner, they hopefully already like her. If not, show them pictures and keep quiet. Let them digest and ask whatever questions they might have. You may be surprised to see that they don't question why Mira is marrying a woman, not a man. If they do, give a simple answer: "People marry the person they love, and Mira loves Susan."

As you talk about it, your kids might want to know if the newlyweds will have kids, and your older child may ask how they could. Again, all you need is a simple explanation of artificial insemination (assuming you've already covered the basics of procreation): "A doctor gives the mother sperm from a man who has given it as a gift, to help them have a baby." They probably know about adoption already, but if not, the relevant explanation is in order.

Now the tough one: telling your kids not to broadcast the information. The key is honesty. You can say: "Some people feel fine about two women or two men getting married, but some people ["including me," if that's the case] don't. In your school, I think many kids and their parents feel it's not right. That's their opinion, and you don't have to agree. And you don't have to tell people about the wedding of you don't want to." Listen to what your kids say and support their right to their opinions while upholding the right of others to differ. The lessons they learn will serve them well as they grow up and navigate the mazes of conflicting views and complex identities.

The Ten Commandments for Grandparents

Several times I have almost literally bitten my tongue when watching my daughter and son-in-law parent. How so? For instance, instead of telling their four-year-old son, "It's time to clean up," they explain for five minutes how important it is to put everything back where it belongs so he can find it tomorrow, how nice it is to have a tidy house, how you must pick up small toys from the floor so that no one trips on them and falls and gets hurt, etc., etc., etc. As they explain, they model by picking up the toys (I guess that, in itself, is a good thing). By the time the explanation is done, they have cleaned up all but one toy. I am so tempted to say something... but I think they'll take offense.

I totally understand both the overall question— "When should you say what?"— and the specific example. I address the very common issue of over-explaining in another chapter ("When 'Parentsplaining' Gets in the Way") and want to focus here on my "Ten Commandments" for being the world's best grandparents.

Commandment 1

You may be grand, but *they* are the *parents*. Always remember who's in charge (not you). Sometimes you'll find it hard to hold back; at other times, you'll be relieved that it's not up to you to deal with a tantrum, hitting, or brazen defiance. Just offer a look of support as you fade into the background.

Commandment 2

Keep your lips mostly sealed. Give advice only when *explicitly asked*, preferably after a second request. If you are asked, there are ways to frame your advice so that it's easier to accept. For example:

1. "What worked for me when you were this age was ___. It might work with Tommy, too."
2. "I see you are trying to get Susie to clean up by explaining how important it is, but it seems she's just ignoring it. Try explaining less and turning it into a game of putting away toys by colors, or shapes, playing I Spy, or make it a hide-

and-seek game: cover your eyes and count to ten and see
how many toys she can put on the shelf while you count."

3. "Sometimes, it's useful to look at your rules/schedule/
expectations and see if it's absolutely necessary to keep it as
is. Maybe you need to think about the situation in a different
way?"

(For more challenging situations, when you feel your grandchild
is being harmed, see the next chapter.)

Commandment 3

Less advice, more empathy. Sometimes what's needed is just an
acknowledgment of how tough it can be, not advice about how to
solve a problem. You can ask, "What's hardest about this issue right
now?" or say, "This is what was hardest for me in dealing with this
kind of situation." It might also help to add, "But I feel like, in my
days as a young parent, we had more permission to mess up, from
ourselves and from the society around us. Your generation seems to
feel like you have to do everything perfectly."

Commandment 4

Offer your time and help with what's needed around the house
besides interacting with the baby or child. Often what helps most
is doing the ancillary, less fun tasks, such as cooking, laundry, and
shopping, to allow the parents to have less pressured time with their
kids.

Commandment 5

Create special grandma/grandpa times and rituals, but let your
kids (and grandkids, as they get older) have most of the control of
when these will take place.

Commandment 6

Discuss with your kids how they want you to set limits when
you're babysitting or taking your grandkids on outings. Get into the
weeds: what rules to enforce and what, if any, may be slightly laxer
with grandparents than with parents (such as extra ice cream or
screen time). Ask what words to use to stop unacceptable behavior,

what should be the consequences for it ("Time out?" Taking away toys or a favorite activity?) and what words to use for the praise of cooperation (being "good" may not be what the parents want you to say, though it does come so naturally).

Commandment 7

Make it possible for the parents to have time off! Having your grandchild over for a sleepover so the parents can have an overnight off is, of course, heavenly. But it may not be practical for a variety of reasons. Start small: a two-hour stint on a weekend afternoon so the parents can go on a walk or out for coffee, babysitting for an hour and a half after bedtime so the parents can go out for an evening stroll or a drink.

Commandment 8

Control your desire to shower your grandkids with presents. If you live in a different town and come for a visit, it's fine, of course, for them to expect a gift when you arrive. But it shouldn't be the Eiffel Tower each time. Ask the parents for their preferences and remember that it might be better to have a *farewell present*, something your grandchild can play with after you leave, that will help them remember you and your visit. As your grandkids grow, think of gifts that can serve as a link between you, such as a board or card game you can play together via phone/video conference.

Commandment 9

For out-of-town grandparents: keep in touch via video conference but respect that your grandkids may grow impatient with "performing" for the camera or iPhone. Instead, make two-minute videos (increasing length as the child matures) of you doing things your grandkid would enjoy watching, such as petting a dog, visiting an educational farm in your town, playing or watching kids playing ball, blooming flowers, even going to the grocery store.

Commandment 10

Take care of yourself too. Don't run yourself ragged babysitting. Your kids need to feel confident that they can ask you to help and get an honest answer about how much you can do. If they think it's too hard on you, they might stop asking even for a little bit of help.

Advice for Grandparents: When You Should Speak Up

Our seven- and nine-year-old grandchildren tell us that their mom (our former daughter-in-law, with whom we never had a good relationship, as hard as we tried) is always yelling at them. Now, when she is not yelling, she is a very engaging, enthusiastic, and loving mom (and, yes, she's been getting counseling for years). The children comment about how peaceful it is at our home and that we handle and resolve problems so amicably (not their word).

How can we, as grandparents, help the kids? Obviously, we don't want to say or do anything insulting to their mom, but we're constantly walking on eggshells. We'd like to subtly offer the grandkids ways to cope. Please help us and other grandparents in our shoes.

As grandparents, you (as well as aunts and uncles and other special adults in a child's life), obviously have a very delicate situation on your hands. It is especially thorny since your rapport with your former daughter-in-law has never been good. You don't say anything about your son's relationship with his kids, his ex, or you, for that matter. If he is involved with the kids and has a halfway decent co-parenting partnership with his ex, he is the key to any possibility of change. He would do well to start by asking his ex-wife to undertake co-parenting training, working with a therapist or coach. He'd best broach this by saying that he feels *he* needs some help and specify one or two parenting dilemmas he'd like to address. In the course of professional support sessions, the yelling can be addressed. If the relationship is too fraught for this course of action, I would expect that there's also no productive way you could talk this through with the mom.

So, what can you do? First, remember that she is your *former* daughter-in-law but will *always* be the mother of your grandchildren. Your first priority is to protect your relationship with the kids, but you need a functioning relationship with their mom for that to be possible. So swallow hard and be ever so careful never to badmouth her. That said, there is a way to, as you say, "to subtly offer the grandkids ways to cope." I would suggest the following:

1. Never forget that visiting grandparents is a bit of a trip to fantasyland: all sweetness and joy. It should stay that way, but it can't (and shouldn't) be like that at home, even with the most wonderful, calm, consistent parents. Setting limits and expectations, enforcing family rules and chores, implementing consequences, all sometimes require parents to be "the bad guys." Grandparents get to be good all the time.

2. When your grandkids comment about how peaceful it is at your house, show them you appreciate it, but also let them know that when you get to your age, with more experience and less pressure, it's much easier.

3. When they talk about their mom yelling, tell your grandchildren something like: "I know it hard/sad/upsetting for you, especially when you see that we try so hard not to yell. We also tried not to yell when your dad was your age. We succeeded a lot of the time, but not always. Some parents yell; some yell a lot. Usually, they don't like it either. I bet your mom doesn't. But they probably don't know how else to get their kids to do what they're supposed to. I know you would do what your mom wants you to even if she didn't yell. Maybe you could tell her that *and show it* by being cooperative."

4. If they seem responsive to the suggestion of saying this to their mother, brainstorm together about how to let mom know they want to be cooperative without offending her (and how to actually be more cooperative).

5. You can gingerly ask if there is someone else they can talk to about this: their dad, or maybe a beloved teacher? Maybe help could come from another direction.

I hope this helps you navigate this difficult road. Of course, if you hear things from your grandkids that suggest abuse going on, whether physical or verbal/emotional, you need to do more. Talk to your son and make sure he takes appropriate action.

PART VI: Make a Book about It

Why Make a Book About It?

Making a book with your child offers you a unique and powerful tool for helping your child cope with difficult and challenging experiences. Creating a book together allows your child to grapple with and master the powerful, often sad or scary emotions the experience evokes. It also enables you to elicit, validate, and support your child's feelings.

All you need to make a book with your child is a pair of child-safe scissors, paste or tape, assorted crayons or colored pencils, a camera (optional), old magazines, this book, and *time*. It can be a lot of fun and a wonderful keepsake, and also an invaluable coping aid. For a young child, the process of making a concrete object by cutting and pasting, drawing, dictating, and writing is much more helpful than reading a ready-made book. A ready-made book, as good as it may be, can leave your child with a sense of how one "ought to feel," while a book made by your child truly validates whatever your child feels. Besides, the open-ended nature of a *Let's Make a Book About It* book allows your child to express genuine, uncensored feelings creatively at their own level.

Often, the book you make together will become a cherished possession, like a security blanket or beloved teddy bear, that magically contains feelings of attachment, caring, and support. You will probably find that your child wants to read the book over and over and will return to it for nurturing and support at other difficult of challenging times. However, some kids may use the book as a way of finishing and putting away the distressing feelings brought up by a difficult event, and that is fine as well.

The following titles are intended for you to cut out and make into a separate book.

Please read the chapter "When a Pet Died" before you get started on this book.

My Pet Died

Let's Make A Book About It

Paste a picture of your pet here.

by Rachel Biale and _____
your name

My Pet Died

Written and Illustrated by
Rachel Biale and _____
(your name)

TRICYCLE PRESS
Berkeley, California

This is me: _____ .

Have your child paste his or her picture and write his or her name on the page (with your help, as needed).

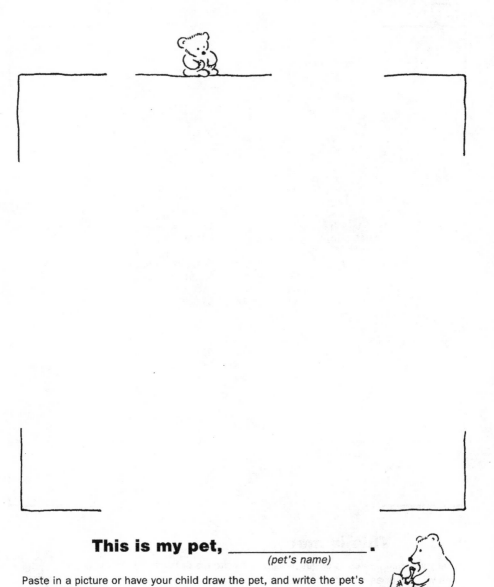

This is my pet, _____.
(pet's name)

Paste in a picture or have your child draw the pet, and write the pet's name on the line.

But _____ died. This is what happened:
(pet's name)

_____

_____

_____

_____

Have your child write or dictate the story of how and where the pet died (at home, at the vet, etc.) If the pet has disappeared or you don't know where it died, have your child still give the place some name such as "somewhere out in the world" or just your town's name. Gently provide your child with explanations and information needed to understand the cause of death, and encourage your child to draw a picture about it. The drawing does not need to be realistic; you can suggest drawing how it *feels,* rather than exactly how it happened.

This is what happened to _____'s body:

(pet's name)

_____

_____

_____

_____

Have your child write or dictate what happened, such as a burial in a pet cemetery or cremation or burial by the vet. If you have a choice, it is preferable from a young child's point of view to bury the pet (even in an unidentified grave) than to cremate it.

Thinking about _____ dying
(pet's name)

makes me feel _____

_____

_____

_____

_____

_____

_____

_____

_____

_____

_____

Have your child write or dictate the feelings on this page and then illustrate them on the facing page with a drawing or pictures. (Illustrations could include magazine clippings or self-portraits.)

 Continue on this page with your child's feelings.

Other people in my family feel _____

_____

_____

_____

_____

_____

_____

_____

_____

_____

_____

 Tell your child how you feel and write it down. Interview everyone in the family and have them either write in the book themselves or dictate their feelings to your child or to you.

_____

_____

_____

_____

_____

_____

_____

_____

_____

_____

Continue with feelings and statements from everyone in the family. Call grandparents (or other extended family members to whom your child feels close) and have them dictate their thoughts over the phone.

I think dying means _____

_____

_____

_____

Have your child write or dictate what he or she thinks death means.
(Hold your input until the next page.) Then have him or her use drawing
and magazine pictures to illustrate these concepts, even if indirectly.
For example, if your child focuses on the body stopping its functions, a
picture of an animal lying down can do. If the focus is on some concept
of "going to heaven" let your child choose how to illustrate it (for instance,
a picture of a beautiful sky, a rainbow, or an abstract design).

My parents told me dying means _____

_____

_____

_____

_____

_____

In simple, clear concepts tell your child how you see death. This is a good time to talk about your religious or spiritual beliefs, or a naturalist-biological view of death. Write it down and illustrate with a drawing or picture. You may want to use an abstract drawing or picture rather than a literal one. Consult the section at the back of this book, "How to Talk to Children About Death," for guidance.

Other people told me about dying that ____

_____

_____

_____

_____

_____

Ask your child whom he or she might want to talk to outside the family to get more information about death. This could include a teacher, a clergy member, the vet, or a trusted friend or neighbor. When you go to talk with these people, take the book along so you or your child can write or draw in it. This is an important part of the process for your child—it involves sharing the news about the pet's death and learning that it is okay to talk about death and ask questions. It also shows your child whom to turn to outside the family.

From books I learned that dying means _____

_____

_____

_____

_____

Have your child write or dictate what he or she may have learned from books about death. (For suggested titles see the reading list at the back of this book.) Illustrate with your child's drawing.

These are other things that I know have died:

_____

_____

_____

Have your child write or dictate a list and illustrate with drawings and pictures. The list can include animals and plants, characters in stories or movies, etc.

This is the story of _____'s life.
(pet's name)

Have your child write or dictate the story of the pet's life from the time you first got the pet. Illustrate with drawings or photos of your pet at different stages. If you do not have photos of the pet use pictures from magazines. Continue on the next page as necessary.

Continue the pet's life story on this page.

This is what I liked most about _____:
(pet's name)

_____

_____

_____

Have your child write or dictate his or her favorite things about the pet. Illustrate with drawings, photos of the pet (if possible), or pictures from magazines of animals doing similar things.

This is what I used to do with _____:
(pet's name)

_____

_____

_____

Have your child describe and draw himself or herself with the pet doing things such as feeding, going on walks, and playing.

If I could talk to _____ I would say

(pet's name)

_____

_____

_____

_____

Have your child write, dictate, and/or illustrate what he or she would say to the pet. Encourage the inclusion of words of farewell.

I know I will be sad for a long time, maybe as long as _____.

Have your child draw and write or dictate about the length of the grieving process. Your child can illustrate this with an abstract drawing or collage, by making a calendar, or by referring to other experiences of time passing.

Here are the people I can talk to when I am sad and I miss _____:

(pet's name)

_____

_____

_____

Have your child write or dictate names of people to talk to, and draw or paste in their pictures.

Here are some things I can do to help myself
when I am sad and I miss _____:

(pet's name)

Have your child write or dictate a list of possible activities and illustrate it with drawings and pictures (such as a picture of the two of you hugging, a picture of a child engaged in a fun activity, etc.). If your child has few or no ideas, you can offer suggestions. (See "Suggested Activities After a Pet Dies for Kids and Parents" at the back of this book.)

I think I'll start feeling better when

_____

_____

_____

_____

_____

Have your child speculate about and then write or dictate what events or passage of time will occur before he or she starts to feel better. A lot of children will say "When I get a new pet." It would be wise to acknowledge the feeling but not rush to do it. Your child needs the time to feel sad and grieve. Ask your child if he or she would like to draw or paste a picture of him or herself looking happy, but do not push it—some children will not be ready yet.

Maybe some day I'll get another pet.

It may be a _____

_____

After some time has passed and you have had a chance to work on all or most of the pages up to this point, have your child write or dictate a list of possible pets and paste in their pictures from magazines. If you are certain that you do not plan to get another pet, skip this and the next page.

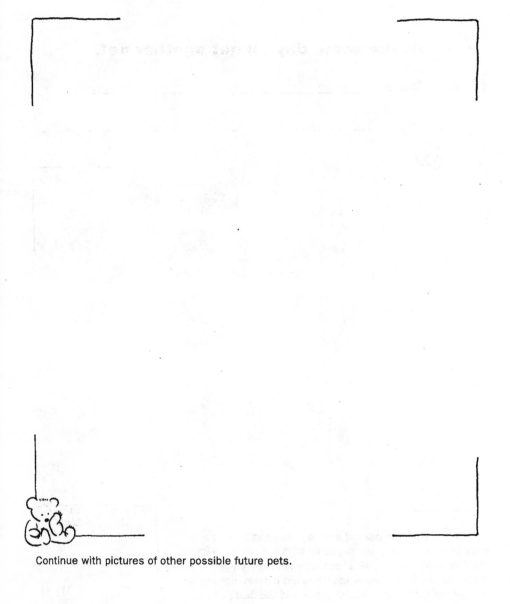

Continue with pictures of other possible future pets.

A long time has passed. Now I feel

_____

_____

_____

About two to four weeks after you've begun work on this book (the older the child, the longer you should wait), have your child write or dictate these feelings and draw a picture to illustrate them.

This is what I would tell other children whose pets die:

_____

_____

_____

_____

Have your child write or dictate words of advice to other children. Illustrate with your child's self-portrait (a drawing or photo) or even a picture of someone teaching children.

Remembering our dog, Papageno

Acknowledgements

Many thanks to Nicole Geiger for her sensitive, thoughtful editing,
and to Brenda Leach for her keen eye and charming design.

TRICYCLE PRESS
P.O. Box 7123
Berkeley, California 94707

Illustrations by Rachel Biale
Book design by Brenda Leach/Once Upon a Design

First Tricycle Press printing, 1997
Manufactured in the United States of America

1 2 3 4 5 6 — 01 00 99 98 97

Please read the chapter "Moving is Hard on Kids" before you get started on this book.

We Are Moving

Let's Make A Book About It

Draw a picture of your family here.

HAND TO MOUSE MOVING COMPANY

by Rachel Biale and _____
your name

We Are Moving

Written and Illustrated by
Rachel Biale and _____
(your name)

TRICYCLE PRESS
Berkeley, California

This is me: _____

Have your child paste his or her picture and write his or her name on
this page (with your help, as needed).

This is my family, the _____ family.

Paste in a picture of the family. In separated, divorced, and blended families, be sure to include both sides of the family and both homes on the next page. Encourage your child also to draw the family and write or dictate to you everyone's names. Include pets.

This is where I live.

Paste a photo and/or have your child draw your home here, and write down your address. You can also include an additional photo and/or drawing of your child's room.

This is my neighborhood.

Take a field trip around your neighborhood with your child and a camera. Take pictures of places and objects your child chooses (including things that may seem insignificant to you). Paste the photos on this page, and help your child draw a map of the neighborhood.

We live in _____
(city/town/village)

Here is what I like about _____.
(town's name)

Visit your town's most prominent sites with your child and a camera. Paste your photos and other pictures from your town's visitors' brochures, guide-books, magazines, etc., on this page.

ENTERING

POPULATION

Here are my favorite places:

Paste in photos of your child's favorite places in town, such as parks and playgrounds and favorite shops, or have your child draw his or her favorites (you can help). Encourage your child to draw or paste pictures of himself or herself next to those sites.

But we are moving to a new home!

Paste in a picture of the new town from a magazine or guidebook, if possible. If you have a photo of your new home, paste it in. If not, draw or clip from a magazine a picture of a similar apartment building or house. Or ask your child to draw the new home as he or she imagines it.

Here is what I know now about our new town.

(I'll know a lot more once we get there!)

It's called _____,

and it's in _____.

("far away" for very young children,
specific state or country for older ones)

Here is what my family has told me about it:

Write down or dictate information about your new town. Use pictures
to illustrate the information, such as if the new place has a beach,
gets snow in winter, is in the mountains, has skyscrapers, etc.

Moving to a new place means

I'll have new _____

List the most important new places for your child, such as a new
preschool, school, or playground. Have your child draw what he or
she imagines these new places would look like and/or paste in
pictures from magazines or newspapers to illustrate.

**Thinking about moving makes me have
all kinds of feelings: some happy,
some sad, and some in-between.**

My happy feelings and hopes are _____

_____

_____

Have your child write or dictate his or her feelings and illustrate with photos of your child
and/or magazine pictures of feeling happy, excited, etc. Encourage your child to show
these feelings by drawing faces or just using colors.

My sad feelings and worries are _____

_____

_____

Repeat exercise on previous page for these feelings.

My parents' feelings are _____

_____

_____

_____

Write down your own feelings (both good and bad) and illustrate
with drawings, photos, or magazine pictures. Change "parents'"
to another term, as appropriate.

Moving means we will pack our things

and put them in a _____
(moving van, car)

and we will _____ **to our new home.**
(drive, fly)

Illustrate how you will relocate with drawings, photos, and
magazine pictures.

Packing means we will _____

_____

_____

_____

_____

Write or dictate how you will pack (who will pack what, what boxes you will use, etc.) and illustrate with drawings and pictures. (Moving company brochures and ads are a good source of pictures.)

Here is what I am taking:

Make a packing list with your child of the possessions your child will be taking using photos, pictures (from toy catalogs and ads), and/or drawings. Write a list with older children.

Here are my own things
that I can't take with me:

Make a list and draw or paste pictures of these things.

Here is what my family is taking:

Make a list and draw or paste pictures of the whole family's important possessions.

This is the way I feel when I leave things behind:

Have your child dictate and draw about the feelings. Talk about saying good-bye to things that are left behind or discarded. Your child may even want to have a little leave-taking ritual (such as throwing a good-bye party for the things left behind, having your child kiss each item good-bye as you pack it away, or donating toys you cannot take with you to needy children).

This is what our family cannot take with us:

Make a list and draw or paste pictures of these things. Include your own feelings about at least one thing you have to leave behind.

These are the people in my family who are moving: _____

_____

 Paste pictures and write names of everyone in the family who is moving.

These are the people in my family who are not moving: _____

_____

Paste pictures and write names of those staying behind, such as grandparents, aunts and uncles, cousins. Skip this page if everyone in the family is moving.

Here are the people in our family and our friends who will be closer when we move:

Paste pictures and write names of family members and friends, if any, you will be closer to after the move, even if they will not be right next door.

Here are the friends I have to leave behind: _____

_____

_____

Paste pictures and write names of your child's friends who will be left behind. Include family friends as well.

Saying good-bye to my friends makes me feel:

Use this space to show how your child feels with photos, drawings, and dictation.

I would like to say good-bye to them like this:

Write down ideas for ways to say good-bye: hugging, a party, etc. Have your child draw or paste a picture to show this. If you have a good-bye party, try to take photos and paste them on this page.

And now we are really moving!

For younger children, paste a picture of your child in motion: running, on a tricycle, in a car. For older children, write the date in large numbers and have your child decorate the page.

On our trip we _____

_____

_____

_____

Have your child write or dictate experiences from the trip
(even a short flight or drive) and illustrate with photos
and postcards from places you visited.

This is my new home:

This is how I feel about it: _____

_____

_____

_____

Work on this page and the one that follows about two weeks after
arrival (sooner with kids under five). Paste photos of your new
home after you have unpacked and encourage your child to express
feelings about the new home, including feelings of missing the old
one. Have your child write or dictate these feelings, and if space
allows, draw or paste pictures to illustrate.

This is my new room:

This is how I feel about it: _____

_____

_____

_____

Repeat the activity from the previous page for your child's new room.

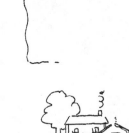

This is our new neighborhood.

Go on several exploration trips in the neighborhood with a camera. Take photos and paste them here with your child's written or dictated description of his or her feelings about the new neighborhood.

This is our new town.

Expand the previous activity to include the town.

These are my new neighbors.

Paste photos or have your child draw pictures of your new neighbors.

This is my new school.

Paste a photo or drawing of your child's new preschool or elementary school, including, if possible, pictures of teachers. Encourage your child to talk about and write down or dictate what he or she likes and does not like about the new school. Skip this page if it is not relevant to your child.

These are my new friends.

Continue the activity from the previous page, allowing a bit more time to pass as your child continues to make friends.

Here is what I think about moving and what I would tell other kids about it: _____

_____

_____

_____

_____

Have your child write or dictate his or her "words of wisdom" about moving. (This works especially well in the format of advice to other kids who move.) Illustrate with a photo or drawing of your child talking to other kids.

Suggested Moving Activities for Kids and Parents

• Play "moving." Use empty cardboard boxes, toy trucks, cars, and planes to play out the process of moving. Encourage your child to play at moving their toys, dolls, puppets, or other figures.

• Play "tourist" in your own community before you leave, taking several trips to explore and photograph favorite and famous places for use in this book. You can make a separate album if you have a lot of pictures and include writing and dictation about these outings as a way of remembering your community.

• With your child's input, plan a good-bye party or other special activity to take place a few days before your departure. Keep the party simple and fun.

• Make multiple photos of your child to give to his or her friends, teachers, etc., before leaving.

• Buy postcards your child would like (your town, animals, etc.) and preaddress them to your new home, including postage. Give them to your relatives, your child's friends, teachers, and neighbors, and ask them to mail them with a brief note within two or three weeks of your departure. Your child will really appreciate the mail, and your friends and relatives will be more likely to do it in this "ready-made" way.

• Prepare with your child a small box or suitcase in which she or he will take the most precious possessions along on the trip. Even if you are loaded down, your child will be very reassured by having these most precious things along at all times. Spend plenty of time with your child planning what to put in this box. If there are too many things, let your child try packing on his or her own to reduce the pile.

• Let your child help with packing, but make the job small and well-defined. Avoid including breakables.

• When you arrive at your new home, make setting up your child's room a priority. Especially for younger children, try to reproduce some of the arrangement of their old room. For example, if your child's bed was under a window in your old place, try to put it under a window in the new one.

• As soon as possible after your move, buy a set of postcards (or, if you can, have a postcard made from a picture of your child in front of your new home) and help your child write out and send them to old friends.

- Put the *We Are Moving* book in a special spot in the new home, and use it frequently as an opening for talking to your child about the move and his or her adjustment.

- Be attentive to your child's needs for consistency and continuity. Before, during, and after the move, try to keep family routines the same. This is especially important with going-to-bed routines and a daily "special time" for close holding and talking with your child. Avoid buying new clothes, toys, and even furniture for your child's room during the transition time; children derive much comfort from their familiar things.

- Read books together that have a character's move as a central theme:

When Grover Moved to Sesame Street, Jocelyn Stevenson (Western Publishing, 1985)

Amelia's Notebook, Marissa Moss (Tricycle Press, 1995; for kids age seven and older)

My Mother's House, My Father's House, C. B. Christiansen (Atheneum Books for Young Readers, 1989; when divorce is the reason for moving)

Dinosaurs Divorce, Laurene Krasny Brown (Little Brown, 1986; when divorce is the reason for moving)

Moving Days, Marc Harshman (Dutton Children's Books, 1994)

Moving, Anita Ganeri (Raintree Steck-Vaughn, 1994)

Moving, Michael J. Rosen (Viking Children's Books, 1993)

Moving with Children, Thomas T. Olkowski and Lynn Parker (Gylantic Publishing, 1995)

Maggie Doesn't Want to Move, Elizabeth Lee O'Donnell (Alladin, 1990)

Recognizing Signs of Stress in Children

Moving can be a very stressful experience for both children and their parents. The following is intended to help parents recognize signs of stress in young children. Remember that you will probably be under considerable stress yourself, which makes it hard to be attentive to and supportive of your child. While you recognize that support, patience, and open communication is what your child needs most, do not be too hard on yourself. Be sure you unwind and get the support you need. The common symptoms of stress listed below can make you feel frustrated, angry, and worried. Try to remain aware of your child's increased needs and the knowledge that this is a temporary transition time.

The symptoms of stress can often be seen through regressions, physical complaints, and emotional disequilibrium. Parents should watch for the following signs:

• Regressing to earlier behaviors such as toileting accidents, thumb sucking, baby talk, needing a bottle, and wanting to be carried.

• Clinging to parents and "love objects" (such as a special blanket, stuffed animal, or pacifier), and difficulties with separations. Also, resisting going to school or new friends' houses, and expressing increased fears and anxieties.

• Sleep disruptions: waking up in the middle of the night, resisting bedtime, needing more parental companionship at bedtime, wanting to sleep in parents' bed, nightmares, and night terrors.

• Physical complaints: stomachaches and headaches are the most common. Other symptoms are loss of appetite and vague complaints about feeling sick along with unusual tiredness. Excessive reaction to minor injuries is also common.

• Increase in temper tantrums, aggression, and wildness will appear in some children, while others become withdrawn and lethargic, or show little or no feeling. Children may express their loss by complaining of boredom and by finding it hard to initiate play. Some show difficulty in concentrating and sustaining their play activities, or seem fidgety and unfocused.

• Increased conflicts with parents and siblings, angry outbursts, and provocative oppositional behavior are very common.

What to Do About Children's Stress

Offer your child your support by making this book, trying the other suggested activities, keeping your daily life simple and your routines consistent, and expressing your certainty that he or she will soon feel more settled and upbeat. Especially with regressive behaviors such as toileting accidents, maintain a balance between assuring your child that the behavior is a common reaction to change, and expressing your certainty that your child will soon regain control and feel as much a "big boy" or "big girl" as he or she felt before the move. If signs of stress persist beyond an initial adjustment period (four to six weeks in children younger than five, and up to two or three months in older children), or if your child has such difficulties that your family life is severely disrupted, it is recommended that you get additional help. Consult a professional, such as a child or family therapist, a pediatrician, or a teacher, for more support and guidance.

For my kids, Noam and Tali

Acknowledgements

I received extremely helpful feedback and wonderful suggestions from Annie Henderson and Malcolm Waugh of Child Education Center in Berkeley, my friends Alan and Abbie Philips, and my husband and kids, David, Noam, and Tali. My friend Mollie Katzen not only gave me excellent ideas and encouragement, but made the initial introduction to my publisher. I wish to thank all of them warmly.

I also wish to thank Nicole Geiger, at Tricycle Press, for her excellent editorial guidance and her warm enthusiasm for the book, and Brenda Leach, the designer, for her delightful work.

Text and illustrations copyright © 1996 by Rachel Biale

TRICYCLE PRESS
P.O. Box 7123
Berkeley, California 94707

Book design by Brenda Leach/Once Upon a Design

First Tricycle Press printing, 1996
Manufactured in the United States of America

1 2 3 4 5 6 — 01 00 99 98 97 96

ACKNOWLEDGMENTS

I am indebted, first and foremost, to the hundreds of parents of young children who trusted me to support and guide them as they navigated common parenting challenges, from babies up every hour to toddlers throwing tantrums and school-age kids still frightened at night. I thank the *J. Weekly*, the San Francisco Bay Area Jewish community newspaper, which published my bi-weekly parenting advice column, *Parenting for the Perplexed*, for over three years. Many of the chapters in this book were first road-tested there. Sue Fishkoff, the *J.*'s editor, supported the endeavor with great enthusiasm and generosity.

I also thank the staff at Publishizer.com, Julia Giurado in particular, for getting me started on this road through their online platform. Appreciation goes to Andrew Hasse who interviewed me on camera and turned a rambling half hour into a concise and compelling two-minute "pitch" for my book (https://publishizer.com/what-now). Just as important were the over one hundred friends, professional colleagues, former consultees, and fellow grandparents who pre-ordered the book via publishizer.com and paved the way to my publisher, Koehler Books. The staff at Koehler Books has brought this book to life: always enthusiastically supportive, meticulous in editing, and creative in design. My thanks to all of them.